Stephanie B. Tansey

Recovery of the Heart

Dialogues with People Working towards a Sustainable Beijing

 NEW WORLD PRESS

First Edition 2012

Written by Stephanie B. Tansey
Edited by Li Shujuan
Cover Design by He Yuting

ISBN 978-7-5104-2634-6

Published by
NEW WORLD PRESS
24 Baiwanzhuang Street, Beijing 100037, China

Distributed by
NEW WORLD PRESS
24 Baiwanzhuang Street, Beijing 100037, China
Tel: 86-10-68995968
Fax: 86-10-68998705
Website: www.newworld-press.com
E-mail: frank@nwp.com.cn

Printed in the People's Republic of China

Foreword

China has the largest indigenous rural population in the world. Now China also has the largest middle class in the world. For seven thousand years we cultivated an agriculture and values-based way of life in rural communities despite limited land and water resources. This had positive externalities that are yet to be recognized. Most developing countries in Asia, like rural China, still have such agricultures as well. Heterogeneous and diverse are important characteristics of an ecological civilization.

In western-centric culture, only a few progressive intellectuals in the West respect and recognize the value of community agriculture in Asia, even when such practices possess the same standards of sustainability and permanence as privatized agriculture. In 1909, Franklin Hiram King (1848–1911), an American agricultural scientist visited Korea and Japan and learned about their agricultural practices and customs. Two years later, in 1911, his pioneering book, *Farmers of Forty Centuries or Permanent Agriculture in China, Korea and Japan* was published which has helped many western private farmers grow sustainably.

One hundred years later, echoing Mr. King's pioneering work, Ms. Stephanie Tansey, through her dialogues with both Chinese and non-Chinese residents of Beijing, encourages us to collaborate with nature as a city in *Recovery of the Heart: Dialogues with People Working towards a Sustainable Beijing*. Ms. Tansey, like Mr. King, has listened and learned from indigenous people on the ground, even though both come from a developed country where developmentalist ideologies are ubiquitous.

Following the 1949 land revolution in China, all arable land in villages was distributed in the form of property rights to all households according to the number of people in the family. This property distribution created a community-based village rationality that could internalize the cost of negative

I

unforeseen effects through the long-term working behaviors within the villages. This village rationality was originally derived from a traditional rural culture that stressed resource sharing, income parity, cooperative solidarity, social justice, and the morality of village elites.

However, in the 1980s, the capitalized government accelerated modernization. Village rationality was gradually replaced by individual rationality, accompanied by the application of reformed social sciences that produced and propagated the capitalized official ideology. The effect was severe pollution.

In 2007 the Chinese central government embarked on the current national strategy of "Ecological Civilization." The government's long-term agricultural policy followed suit in 2008 seeking to create "resource conserving and environmentally friendly agriculture." Unfortunately there have been problems and failures.

The intent of this book is to demonstrate that individual Beijingers do deeply support the idea of a sustainable city. Sustainable agriculture is an important way to repair human relations with mother earth. Fair trade is the way to construct the foundation for the rural-urban solidarity needed to encourage a sustainable society. Also important are communal skills so citywide common resource allocations and problems can be resolved through dialogues. Betsy Damon's delight at finding living water communities, and Jim Spear's encounters in Mutianyu, highlight a history of oriental rationality in rural communities in the past. I believe that today a new oriental rationality that includes conversations between grassroots people, intellectuals, and even expats with good listening skills, can move us towards our ecological civilization.

We very much need the solidarity this book proposes. China now has the largest number of pro-food safety and pro-ecology advocates in the world. As shown by Wang Zhiqin and Yang Jing, ordinary people want to connect to nature again. Together, we could create a fair trade-based sustainable consumption campaign that would transform our cities. Beijing should lead the way.

Wen Tiejun
Dean
School of Agricultural Economics & Rural Development
Renmin University of China

Contents

Introduction.. 001

Navigating East/West Dialogue: China and the U.S. 027

Acknowledgements... 031

Mac Fan, the Everyman 032

Little Donkey Farm, Creating Farm to Fork, Step by Step 052

Yang Ke, A Platform for Public Dialogue 075

Jim Spear, Sustainable Tourism, Building Design and the 21st Century Village 096

Professor He Huili, the Rice Professor from China Agriculture University 119

Wang Zhiqin, Taiji Rouliqiu Teacher, Connected to Nature, Naturally........................... 136

Therese Zhang Zhimin, Human Beings and Nature, and the Art of Agriculture 153

Yang Jing, Kites and Culture, Balancing the Traditional and the Fresh 175

Betsy Damon, Visionary for a Living Water Sustainable Future..................................... 192

Beijing as a Sustainable Society 211

Resources 227

Glossary 230

Notes 235

Credits for Illustrations 239

Introduction

The purpose of this book is to open up a dialogue with citizens here in Beijing and around the world. We are already doing things that make our cities environmentally more sustainable. The citizens in this book are like you. They, like you, have a passion for what they do. They, like you, know who they are and where they are going.

We won't always see this dream come true in our lifetime. The day all urban residents pay farmers a good price at the market so rural children can get a good education. When farmers can revel in being honest and hardworking instead of using chemical fertilizers to make ends meet. We can all work, though, towards a time when people lead meaningful lives that are enriched by our relationship with nature.

The future will be far better because we are here now. Our water will run pure and fresh and invigorate life with new purpose. People will welcome waste treatment centers to their neighborhoods. Someday the local villages around Beijing will become places where citizens make wise lifestyle choices and live sustainably on the land. Beijing will become a healthy place to raise children.

More and more people, passionate about a personal hobby that connects them to the sustainable needs of their city, will take the time, purposefully, through art, culture, and great conversations, to reconnect themselves to earth and their society and begin to look forward to taking part in the grand idea of becoming a sustainable society, because they want balance in their lives again.

The people in this book are not here for the short term. They are success stories because they think about being part of the process. They are common people just like you. They are self-educated or formally educated. Some have left good jobs to pursue a dream. They thrive on the idea that they are making a difference, and that the future will be better.

Most of them are Chinese, but not all. Beijing is a crossroads, just as it has been for many thousands of years. Though now gigantically bigger. Some people are here from somewhere else in China because they got into good universities here. Others were born here. Some stay for a while and then go home. Some work outside of government, others inside it.

I like to think of each of them as an Everyman. An Everyman means an ordinary person who depicts the human being in extraordinary circumstances. This is a Western term but I think we should have a global way to describe people like this who can be found, of course, all over the world. Such people are individuals out to help their society in times of crisis. Let's call these people "Everyhumans." Each will be familiar to you in some way.

To think that Beijing is going to become a sustainable city is extraordinarily idealistic at the moment. Beijing is running out of water. A place once awash with river water is now dry as a bone. Good and bad decisions made in Beijing affect not only the wellbeing of its citizens and the environs of Beijing Municipality, but also send messages out to other cities.

Just like in capitals and great cities around the world, Beijing Municipality weighs the impact of policy decisions against a complex set of priorities. I do not condone corruption. I am angry when I see stupidity and greed. But I also recognize these in other capitals and cities elsewhere. This book is not where you are going to find justice for such bitter fruit.

The Art and Power of Dialogue

People don't believe in the power of dialogue today. But we have in the past. For example, Shakespeare in *Hamlet:*

What a piece of work is a man, How noble in Reason, how infinite in faculties, in form and moving how express and admirable, In action how like an Angle! In apprehension how like a god, the beauty of the world, the paragon of animals.

The cry of man so angry, but at the same time an infinite call towards what we can be.

As witnessed in the Tang Dynasty in China, the Heian Period in Japan, the European renaissance, the Hindu renaissance, and the American renaissance, and certainly among indigenous peoples around the world in Africa and the Americas – when what it means to be human, connects with art, that dialogue is transformational.

The dialogue between these Chinese Everyhumans and yourselves is an important one. Chinese culture nurtures a consciousness that contains a certain wisdom that is distinctive and old. We can say that they have on glasses with different colored lenses than ours. While Americans may have blue lenses on, Indians pink ones, Russians green. What is important to realize is that Chinese lenses are red. You think they see the world in a blue/pink/green light but they do not. They think you see red but you do not.

Although my glasses are sometimes opaque no matter what the color, I have been lucky because some friends have let me inside China. I also was born and raised in Asia, in Japan, and have been a Buddhist for many years so I am familiar with some of the values implicit in why Chinese think the way they do. Not always, as you will see from this book. There are others whose lenses seem to be able to blend or change colors, and they can see from both perspectives. I have learned much from them.

Now that Beijing has become such an important place in the world, we all have to find a way to see life from the Chinese perspective too. Or to have a set for "reading" people who are not like us. We both have to work hard at this.

Much of what Beijingers say is implicit, just as only New Yorkers and Londoners, and Parisians, and Tokyoites understand what undercurrents are going on in their city and in the ethos of their culture. Add to this the last 60 years as the capital of the People's Republic of China, much of it isolated from the world, and you can understand that this inside world and our outside world grew up very differently after World War II.

For this reason I have added a brief history of Beijing and its relationship with the land beneath it. I also have added some of the most fundamental values that Chinese philosophy possesses, which can have a positive impact on the environment of the future. I have left out others that are more familiar but don't have such a bearing on how Chinese think intrinsically about nature and the role this can play in conceptualizing a sustainable society.

At the same time, fresh ideas from inside and outside of China, have been streaming into Beijing since before Huangdi became the father of the Chinese people, and they continue to impact the values, cultural traditions and economic reality of Beijing. Jicheng, Yanjing, Zhongdu, Dadu, Peking or what is now Beijing, has always been a place where many cultures and ideas mixed together. Ideas about humanity, culture, writing, music, poetry, as well as advances in agriculture, science, technology and communication. New ways of designing resulted. New engineering ideas. New ways of doing business, and new inventions.

Perhaps we can think about sustainable cities in the same way. After all, cities are all going to have to become sustainable. It is no longer possible to think, with water resources so low in the world, with pollution so pervasive, and population climbing, that we can do anything else. It is only a matter of when, and where, that tipping point will occur first.

A city is a living organism. Like all of life, it exists as part of an ecosystem. You can forget this, you can tamper with it and/or reshape that ecosystem if you like, but to be healthy, life has to come from a healthy ecosystem. We can either be the tipping point, or have the tipping point come from nature. So here are some best practices in Beijing, and let's think about how they fit into the global roadmap to the tipping point that we want to see, the one we create ourselves. These are not the only models, of course, but they are a good place to begin.

Human Beings, the Land and the Culture

People have been living here for 710,000 years. Beijing sits on an alluvial plain rimmed with mountains on the west (Western or Xishan Mountains) and northwest and north (Jundu Mountains). The plain tilts as it goes towards the Bohai Sea to the southeast.

The mountains shield the land and inhabitants from the desert sands of the Gobi Desert. Major rivers flowing through the municipality include the Yongding River and the Chaobai River, which is part of the Hai River system. Both flow from northwest to southeast. There are also several smaller rivers. Once it became the capital, it was the northern terminus of

Peking Man 755,000 years ago

The hill in Fangshan County where Peking Man lived

the ancient Grand Canal that began in Hangzhou, near Shanghai. The Miyun and Huairou Reservoirs are crucial to the water supply.[1] They feed the lakes inside the city as well.

But before it was the capital of China, it was the capital of smaller states. Before that it was home to nomads from the north, and before that to Neolithic peoples and before that to Paleolithic human beings 710,000 years ago.

Peking Man, as he is known, his family and clan members, lived in caves in the mountains that are the southwestern border of Beijing. This is now Fangshan District. These first humans enjoyed many of the same things that later people enjoy. At least until the development of Beijing as a big walled city.

It was an inter-glacial period, so slightly warmer than today. The mountains were full of trees and he and his family gathered nuts – hazel, pine, elm were good to eat, as were rose seeds. On the grasslands (which is now the city) he hunted several kinds of deer and smaller animals. Peking Man was a cave dweller, toolmaker, fire user, gatherer, and hunter. Viewing fossil records and cultural remains, he was superb in adapting himself to his environment both physiologically and creatively.

Bronze Steamer in Yan Dynasty
(Capital Museum)

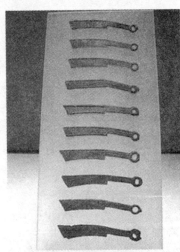

Sword-shaped Yan coins
(Capital Museum)

When he died out (no one knows why), Neolithic peoples came and settled around the plain – up in the north around the Changping area as well as in the south as before. Millet agriculture began about 7000 BCE. They developed the ability to store and redistribute crops, and had specialized craftspeople as well as a social and political order. They drew pictographs mainly of grazing animals, agriculture and hunting, perhaps to pass these skills on to their young.

The Ji people, part of the Han culture, lived in their town, Jicheng. Dongjialin, where the Yan people, also Han, lived just to the southwest, had another center. Eventually in the 11th century BCE, the Yan overthrew the Ji. The State of Yan set up its capital at Jicheng, because it was closer to the Yongding River. Lotus Lake and wells supplied water for daily life. Yanjing beer is still a favorite beer in Beijing today.

It was a prosperous market town. The river irrigated the crops. The hunting and foraging were good. The river, though turbulent, had abundant fish. The forests were full of trees. Traders came back and forth over the mountains going south and east. These two trade routes continued to be important.

In 221 BCE the Emperor, Qin Shihuang, established the first unification of China and set up his capital in Xianyang in Shaanxi to the west. Jicheng/Yanjing ceased being a capital and became just a prefectural town, though an important trading center. The Qin Dynasty (221-206 BCE) unified China but did not last long.

Emperor Qin was concerned about invasions from nomads to the north from the Xiongnu empire. He ordered the building of a new wall to connect some older fortifications along his newly acquired mountain ranges to the north. Thousands of people died putting up this Great Wall over the centuries. It was completed by the Ming in the 16th century.[2]

In the Sui Dynasty (581-618) the trading center became known as Zhuojun. During the Tang Dynasty (618-907), it was renamed Youzhou and became a military outpost. During the Tang Dynasty, it supplied troops as they headed east to the kingdoms in Korea and back. It has remained part of military districting ever since.

In the 10th century, the Khitan, a Mongolian tribe from the western Liao River area in northern China, established the Liao Dynasty in 907. In 936 they occupied Youzhou and named it Nanjing (Southern Capital). It became a secondary capital for the Liao Dynasty. In 938, the city became one of the five capitals of the Kingdom of Liao (947-1125) and the city was renamed Yanjing.

What was life like during this time on the plain? Rice was now cultivated in the marshlands to the east. Handicrafts, pottery, cloth and cooking materials supplied the residents of the city with goods. Workmanship continued to develop. Writing and computation were clearly necessary for the trading of goods. Feeding and clothing of the soldiers, providing for campaigns, entertainment and culture promoted the development of the city.

The farmers and their villages were much the same as before. They fed and clothed the city dwellers. The farmers needed nature to favor them, so rites, agricultural knowledge, and ancient wisdom which connected to the rhythms of nature were important to them. The connection with farmers and city folk was driven by personal relationships and fostered by living close to the land. Government taxes were also part of life as well, but at this point the emperor was far away and disconnected from the local land.

The people inside the city were more cosmopolitan. They were merchants, craftsmen and gentry. Music, dance, food and entertainment were all part of city life. New peoples and ideas mixed into Chinese culture. Buddhism

Niujie, the oldest mosque in Beijing, was founded in 996.

in particular, spread from the south, taking hold in the city and then headed east to Korea and Japan, and north to the Mongols. Buddhist temples now dotted the landscape, intermingling with shrines and temples of Christian sects, Muslim beliefs, Taoism and Confucianism.

The Jin Dynasty (1115–1234) was the next big step. The Jurchen, a people from the north, swept south, created an empire and established their capital on the same plain, now called Zhongdu. They improved water conservancy. Though some of their water projects failed, Lugouqiao (known to the West as the Marco Polo Bridge), has stood the test of time.[3]

The Jin Dynasty was short-lived, falling to the Mongols and Genghis Khan. Picture this: You are on the walls of the city looking north. There are huts below and people are cooking and getting ready for dinner. You look north and feel a rumbling. A huge shadow on the plain appears. All of a sudden you realize that shadow are soldiers on horses. Thousands of them heading right towards you. The air becomes filled with panic as you and the small number of soldiers get ready to defend the city and begin to pour from the city. The farmers in their huts outside the city walls race towards the huge mass in front of them with whatever they have in their hands. It is hopeless, of course. The Horde has arrived.

The first Mongol siege of Dadu/Beijing (1213-1214). The city fell in the second siege (1214-1215).

Yuan Emperor Kublai Khan made Beijing his capital.

This is the video that the Capital Museum in Beijing shows visitors about the arrival of the Mongols. A good example of what all Asia and parts of Europe experienced. The Yuan Dynasty (1271-1368) with Kublai Khan, grandson of Genghis Khan, as emperor ruled from Beijing, which was now called Dadu. They improved agriculture, encouraged trade along the Silk Road, built highways and granaries and promoted science and religion. Visits from other parts of Asia and from the West began to be part of everyday life. After the death of Genghis Khan, the subsequent emperors never had the same power and eventually lost the support of the people.[4]

From the Yuan Dynasty to modern China, more and more people were drawn to this plain and its growing metropolis. Water supply continued to be a problem.

During the Ming Dynasty (1368-1644) the population of China was about 180 million. Ming rule, with its vast navy and legendary tributary fleet under the Muslim eunuch Admiral Zheng He in the 15th century far surpassed all others in size. There were enormous construction projects, including the restoration of the Grand Canal and the Great Wall and the establishment of the Forbidden City in Peiping (Beijing) during the first quarter of the 15th century.

The Ming attempted to create a society of self-sufficient rural communities in a rigid, immobile system that would have no need to engage with the commercial life and trade of urban centers. This rebuilding of China's agricultural base and strengthening of communication routes had the unintended effect of creating a vast agricultural surplus that could be sold at burgeoning markets located along courier routes. Rural culture and commerce became influenced by urban trends. The upper classes embodied in the schol-

Ming Emperor Yongle moved the capital to Beijing in 1421.

arly gentry class were also affected. Even merchant families began to produce examination candidates to become scholar-officials and adopt the style of the noblemen.[5]

The Qing (1616-1911) were also Jurchen, like the Jin. They were isolationists. Their capital was again Beijing. They spent much of their time putting down rebellion after rebellion. Their empire began to stagnate, and Western nations began to take advantage of this. They disliked the idea of trade with the West since there was nothing they really needed from them. Western nations added opium to their list of goods, grown in India and other colonies, and the result was the development of rampant use of opium. This led to continued stagnation and to the end of the empire. It also put an end to this form of government. The Qing mostly built gardens and parks. At first the Westerners helped them build these projects, including the Summer Palace or Yuanmingyuan, adding splendid Western architectural masterpieces. However, in 1860 and in 1900 the Anglo-French Allied Forces and the Eight Imperialist Powers, respectively, invaded Beijing and destroyed the park to show the Qing who was in charge. Today, the park is visited by scores of students every year (like Pearl Harbor and others) so the young can understand and remember what China has suffered from foreign invaders.[6]

At the beginning of the 20th century Beijing began to grow more. Universities were established. Trade with the West and domestic trade made the

Foreign armies in Beijing in 1860

Yuan Shikai moved the capital to Beiping/Beijing in 1912.   Sun Yatsen (1866-1925)

city a market center at an entirely new level, and this influenced political reform, science, religion and culture. It was a new kind of capital.

In 1911 the Republic of China was established by Sun Yatsen (Sun Zhong-shan) in Nanjing. He ceded his presidency to Yuan Shikai in return for helping oust the Qing. Yuan moved the capital back to Beijing. He used his army and pre-existing warlords to gain control of the new country.

During this period, Beijing started to become a modern metropolis. The city's population grew from 725,235 in 1912 to 863,209 in 1921. The municipal government built public works including paved and widened streets, created parks, installed trolley service, and began urban planning. They built modern water utilities, improved sanitation and the health of the population.

The warlords battled each other until the Kuomintang Army succeeded in pacifying them. Nanjing became the capital in 1928. Beijing was renamed Beiping.

When Japan invaded and occupied the city in 1937, many universities relocated. Anti-Japanese resistance fighters began to get assistance from Communist partisans who were waging guerrilla warfare in rural outlying areas. The official surrender of Japanese forces took place on October 10, 1945, in the present capital, now renamed Beijing.

Civil War broke out in 1948 between the Nationalists and Communists who wanted to liberate China from entrenched feudalism and Western imperialism. The U.S. government's emissary, George C. Marshall, tried to broker a truce and a coalition government but this ultimately failed. Beiping was the army headquarters of the Nationalists. In 1949, four years later, the People's Liberation Army surrounded the city and the Nationalists were defeated.

The Communist Party of China (CPC) grew out of the May 4th Movement of 1919 in Beijing. On that day, massive student demonstrations shook Beiping and grew into a nationwide movement. It was here that Li Dazhao first disseminated Marxism in China. Where Mao Zedong grew into his leadership role, developing strategies, training personnel and capturing the support of the peasants. It is also where the great writer and thinker Lu Xun began, with his pen, to awaken the hearts of the Chinese people out of their apathy and oppression from the Qing, feudalism and foreign imperialism.

In this way ancient Jicheng became the birthplace of revolution in modern China. On October 1, 1949, in Beijing, Chairman Mao Zedong proclaimed, "The Chinese people have stood up!" All of the palaces, in Beijing and around China, were made into the people's palaces and parks. Public education was established for the first time, and finally for the women, who according to Mao, "hold up half the sky," the law forbidding foot-binding was enacted.

As the capital of the People's Republic of China, Beijing wanted their capital to reflect the new kind of society they hoped to build. Two million people came to Beijing at that time to help build it.

In the Soil of Chinese Civilization Today

5000 years ago to the west and the south of the plain that Beijing sits on, Chinese civilization began along the Yellow River.

Time is not as linear to Chinese as it is for people from the West. Chinese characters are pictographs that eventually became characters. Each part of a character means something that when put together becomes a concept. For example, "'Home' is where I live." "'家' 是我住的地方 ." Each part of "home" helps create the idea of home. In the same way, time can be flexed to create an important concept as well.

The Yellow Emperor (Huangdi) is believed to be the father of the Chinese people. Whether Huangdi lived or is a just a legend, is not important. What is important is that from the "Huangdi concept," which arose around 2704 BCE in Shaanxi, came the introduction of wooden houses, carts, boats, the bow and arrow, and writing. Some traditions also credit him with the introduction of governmental institutions and the use of coined money. The concept "Huangdi's wife" discovered sericulture (silk production) and taught women how to breed silkworms and weave fabrics of silk.[7]

There was another very important contribution. Huangdi had a dream. He dreamed that in the future an ideal kingdom would develop and peaceful descendants would live in harmony with the natural law. Chinese call this Datong (大同) or the Great Harmony.

On waking from his dream, Huangdi sought to inculcate the virtues of order and shared prosperity, to start his people on their journey to Datong. Because of this dream, people made him an immortal. This story has been handed down generation after generation for these 5,000 years. It is still taught to children in China today, although many feel it is a distant ideal at best.

Shennong (Divine Farmer), who "lived" at the same time, is considered the father of agriculture. Many people were sickly, hungry and diseased. He taught them how to cultivate the soil wisely. He invented the plow, the rake and the noonday market. He also is renowned as the father of Chinese Traditional Medicine. He is said to have tasted hundreds of herbs to test their attributes. When some were poisonous, he would then take others until he cured himself. Tea was one of the herbs he took to cure himself. Shennong is also considered a father of the Chinese people because he introduced them to the art of agriculture, the art or fusion of man and nature.[8]

From here the Chinese wove a culture. Beginning with the Xia (2070-1600

BCE) and then the brutal Shang Dynasty (1600-1046 BCE) and the Zhou Dynasty (1045-256 BCE).

The authoritarian form of absolutist rule was established with the Shang, along with bronze art, divination and writing. During the Zhou, China developed into the highly developed, distinctive civilization it is today.[9]

Confucius (551-479 BCE) was born during the Zhou Dynasty. He gathered up all the wisdom from ancient traditions and selected from them a way forward. The four books, *The Book of Songs, The Book of Rites, The Doctrine of the*

Confucian Temple built in Beijing 1302

Mean, and *I Ching*, from the mixing bowl of peoples, ideas and traditions and became a vibrant part of Chinese culture.

His philosophy was about personal growth and responsible government. *The Book of Songs* shows how to live and rule wisely. *The Book of Rites* is how to best connect with nature. *The Doctrine of the Mean* teaches how to be an exemplary human being. The *I Ching* describes how change happens, enabling a person to locate the way forward.

One of the pre-Chinese concepts is Datong (大同).[10] Confucius was concerned that his principles would be taken too practically. How to advance in your career, for example. This was not what he wanted to convey. Being socially and politically responsible is the real learning. To do this, we must become the master of ourselves. If people can have such self-mastery, he believed that society could attain that ideal kingdom, through living life well. This is not an end but a dynamic process. This is not uniformity; it is the harmony of differences – looking for agreement with people who do not think alike. It is collaboration.

The Doctrine of the Mean, the third of the Four Books, is of particular interest because it says that anyone can become *junzi* (君子), just as anyone can become an Everyhuman if "they depict the human being in extraordinary circumstances."

Such an exemplary man, a *junzi*, is someone who acts in the Mean at all times. Most people believe that they cannot be *junzi*, and certainly not *junzi* all the time. But the Chinese know a person who is *junzi* when they see one, and would want to be one if they felt they could.

E.R. Hughes in his *Chinese Philosophy in Classical China*, writes, "In Chinese there is no 'doctrine.' There are just two words, one *chung* (*zhong*), meaning normally 'the centre,' but here more probably approximating what philosophers mean by 'the Mean;' the other, *yung* (*yong*), the word used for denoting a common workman or the tasks which such a man performs. The idea, therefore, seems to be that of a Mean to be found in all types of action. Since the material universe is included in the author's purview, 'the Mean inaction' is about as near to the Chinese as we can get."[11]

In today's world I'd like to think that being *junzi* is like becoming a better and better global citizen. You don't get there all at once. One day you realize that you need to care more about the environment. Then at some point you want to. Then you start changing your behavior, your opinions, or you take concrete actions. In this way you add and add to how you act. At some point you want others to encourage still others. This then has a multiplier effect, and transformation occurs.

In *The Book of Songs*, there is an ode, "The Reluctant Warrior," which can help us understand what is in the hearts of the people in Beijing. They have been a part of, as you have read, many, many wars. For the same land, over and over again. The description of the Chinese warrior's parting grief is implicit and suggestive. He is reluctant to go to war, but his feeling is revealed through the willows' sadness.

> When I left here,
> Willows shed tears.
> I come back now;
> Snow bends the bough.[12]

The Book of Songs served as education for intellectuals for thousands of years. Here we have the symbol of willows weeping, implying the harmony between man and nature. He is reluctant to go to war but must do his duty. In Chinese philosophy, to have to go to war implies a lack of wisdom, an inability to live with people whose ideas are different. In this way, the Book taught the man-nature connection and social harmony based on respect for different approaches that became a philosophical undercurrent in Chinese history.

It doesn't mean that just because it is an ideal that the Chinese were able to refrain from war. Like people from the West, they have not always been able to live their ideal, and failed to be the master of their mind. Laozi, a contemporary of Confucius, also took up this connection with nature. Tao is the source of all nature. There are two forces that interact and cause change (creation) in nature. These forces are *yin* and *yang*. *Yin*, which is the Mandarin word for moon, represents the female, darkness, wetness, coolness. *Yang*, which is the Mandarin word for sun, represents the male, lightness, dryness, heat. The tension between *yin* and *yang* causes endless change through production, reproduction and the transformation of energy. *Yin* and *yang* bring about change and balance in life, and their interaction is the cause of all creation. From the synergy between farmer and agriculture, to the rulers, who were the mediators between nature and man, everyone supported the idea that human life must fit into nature's rhythms.

Taoists believe that the universe is hierarchically organized in such a way that its entirety is reproduced in its individual parts. Thus, man is a micro-cosm within the macrocosm (small universe within a larger one). All is from the Tao, and all will return to the Tao. We are here to reunite with the Tao through a transformation from disharmony to harmony.[13]

Buddhism was introduced in China around 100 CE. Buddhism spread from India as well as from Central Asia. The translations into Chinese took some time finding their rightful place in the culture. However, once it was well translated, Chinese welcomed the idea of compassion as a way to enlightenment. Indeed Zhongdu/Beijing was an early center. Development of compassion led to the ability to see the true reality, and through the ability to perceive it, you could bring forth your own enlightenment. According to Buddhism, every human being has a relationship with society and with the natural environment. The deeper the polishing of your true self, the more you can help others and fuse with the natural environment, the more enlightened you become. This also causes transformation of the environment.

Thus integration between human beings and nature and the common ideal Datong became part of the Chinese ethos in these different ways. This is not always conscious, and with the focus on a market economy, the ancient values may now be buried deep. But they are not dead. These hidden values are far easier to connect with than ones imposed from outside.

Sun Yat-sen, the father of modern China, wanted to cultivate such a culture of peace. Part of Zhou Enlai's basic philosophy was to work towards peaceful co-existence.

When social harmony was disregarded, as during the Cultural Revolution, there was disaster. Learning from this disaster, the CPC turned to gradualism as the best way for reform. Testing policies in real society to determine which ones work best is the better way to move towards a future Datong. Once people have enough hope and the wellbeing to believe in such things, this could be said to be how China sees its road ahead.[14]

These two ideas, social harmony through diversity and the oneness of man and nature, were always the educational foundation of the life of common people, mostly the peasants and merchants. They didn't have any formal education. They used the ancient stories and principles of living to maintain their own health, and work together to get things done in the village. The most important factor in deciding anything even today, in thousands of villages, even with some public education, starts from such lessons from the past.

In New China, the egregious destruction of the land, water and air, and the gap between the urban and the rural, deeply concerns people today, in and out of government. Everyone can feel this imbalance, except for those infected by consumerism. They are both common topics for netizens.

China and the Beijing Municipality are very serious about addressing the problem but to do so, industry, trade, the supply systems and the people have to want to do it too. China is also part of another environment – the global one – and their economy is dependent on the world's economy. Everyone understands that there is a grave imbalance. There is an approved Beijing City Master Plan already under way.

Modern China and the Wisdom of Socrates

The People's Republic of China in 1949 realized that it had to industrialize if it didn't want to be conquered again. Universities developed and students went abroad to learn from the West and Japan. Industrializing agriculture, damming rivers for electricity, mining to create steel were the priorities needed to remain independent from Russia and other foreign states. Confucius and other ancient value systems were discarded for socialist ideals.

After the Cultural Revolution, Deng Xiaoping opened up the economy, and business developed. The parts of modern society that drive a market economy also promote consumerism, advertising, and mass production without sufficient controls. Factories abused workers and spewed toxins into their water systems. As the economy went into high gear, China was able to put in transportation infrastructure, rebuild cities, create an auto industry, and design highly sophisticated technology. It was blind to the effects on human health, human dignity, and the environment. It was the wild, wild West but this time on the eastern side of the Pacific.

When China woke up to the reality of the mess it had created, it turned to the West for answers. The Chinese were no longer sure what place, if any, their own ancient values had in this new world. Much of their thinking, from medicine to farming, was laid aside for modern methods. Of greatest concern, and particularly in Beijing, was that such industrial destruction made potable water, precious in any country these days, a significant problem for large segments of the population.

In the last 20 years, Beijingers have become more and more concerned about the food they eat. Milk scandals were just the beginning. Chemicals in the meats. GMO products sold as normal produce. Over-spraying of fruits with pesticides. At the same time, cancers, lifestyle illnesses and obesity have sharply increased. Beijing is not the first city nor is the PRC the first nation to experience this awakening to the reality of food as a business.

Recently China was the subject of a very interesting study which has served as notice to the rest of the world about how to eat well for your health, and it is making its way into Chinese society as well. *The China Study*, by T. Colin Campbell and Thomas M. Campbell II, in 2006 came out with a report from its findings. They studied the effect of increased meat on the people of China. It was the most comprehensive study of diet, lifestyle and disease ever done with humans in the history of biomedical research. It was jointly organized by Cornell University, Oxford University and the Chinese Academy of Preventive Medicine.

The project ran 20 years in the 70s and 80s and surveyed diseases, diet and lifestyle factors in rural China. It produced the finding that people who ate the most animal-based foods got the most chronic diseases. Why did they do this in China? Because the Chinese were one basic ethnic group (Han) and they've been basically eating locally grown, whole foods for centuries. They were also poor, and so many ate very little meat, until now.

People who ate plant-based foods were the healthiest, and Campbell showed that chronic diseases – heart disease, diabetes, and obesity – could be reversed by going back to whole foods. Various cancers, autoimmune diseases, bone health, kidney health, vision and brain disorders are convincingly influenced by diet as well.

Indeed, it appears cities and nations have had such ongoing problems for quite some time. Campbell has a wonderful dialogue from Plato. Socrates and Glaucon, talk about diet and what cities should do to have healthy residents.

In this 2,500-year-old dialogue, Socrates believes cities should be simple and people should eat whole foods, topped with salt, olives, cheese and such, fruits and roasted nuts for dessert and wine, of course. But Glaucon feels that it would be boring to have a life without meat. Socrates replies that if you introduce the "luxury" of meat, then there will be inflammations in the body. You will need a lot of animals as well. So then you will need medical men and a lot of land. This will lead to discriminatory acts, which could lead to violence and then war. And then you will need not only doctors, but also lawyers and judges. So in this luxurious city of sick and angry people, it will be normal to have many doctors and lawyers.[15]

"Though it is indeed remarkable that one of the greatest intellectuals in the history of the Western world condemned meat-eating almost 2,500 years ago, I find it even more remarkable that few know about this history. Hardly anybody knows, for example, that the father of Western medicine, Hippocrates, advocated diet as the chief way to prevent and treat disease."

"How did Plato predict the future so accurately? He knew that consuming animal foods would not lead to true health and prosperity but only to... a culture of sickness, disease, land disputes, lawyers and doctors."[16]

It seems as if cities are universally plagued by disease, land disputes, lawyers and doctors. To create sustainability in Beijing, residents have to *want* to make such choices. Of course the meat industry has found ways to limit the size of pastures, but not the amount of land it takes to feed the animals. We can choose to support the ecosystem and eat less meat. We and our families will be healthier. We can do this to support the lives of our children's families and the city where they will live. What is a choice for our generation, may not be for the next one.

Globalization, China and Fresh Ideas

In our brief spin through history and philosophy, there is one vital area that has not been mentioned enough: fresh ideas.

Throughout Chinese civilization and intrinsic to Beijing has been the influx of new ideas, new people, new cultures. The dynasties are full of different cultures sitting on the throne. Indian, Vietnamese and Thai, Central Asians, Mongolians, Tibetans, people of Russia, Arabs, Africans, Japanese, Koreans and more have traveled back and forth along the Silk Road for centuries, bringing in and taking out ideas with their trades.

Some of the "real" Beijingers today are Muslim from the Jin and the Yuan dynasties. Folklore, Chinese philosophy, outside influences, mass culture and inter-civilization dialogues continue to take place, in many forms. All are part of modern Beijing. Many Chinese have cast aside the past and are chasing the golden calf of capitalism. Some are already looking for better balance. They are all part of Chinese culture.

Beijing was and is a great bazaar of life. Today's cultural Silk Road is vibrant, and the cyberspace Silk Road, despite the Wall, is an important influence. The world is coming to them as more and more foreigners sign up at *Weibo* (Chinese Twitter) and weigh in on discussions of all kinds.

Then there are the differences and the problems – between classes, provincial and minority biases. War histories, invasions, corruption, slavery, health and environmental calamities, and migrations of workers into the city. This has been going on for 5,000 years. It makes you understand why Chinese people want peace and harmonious relations. Why China always suggests dialogue. Why Sunzi said that use of hard power means you have already lost.

To date globalization has been very destructive to the planet and to people. When I think of why, I always go back to the Industrial Revolution. I have lived in Central Asia, Central America, the Middle East and Sub-Saharan Africa, besides China, Japan, and North America. I have seen communities devolving because of the focus on the individual without concern for the human dignity of the Other. Perhaps the true damage was that the West harnessed the Industrial Revolution to Social Darwinism – that some people were just superior to others. Survival of the fittest. When nature is about balance.

However, there are ways in which globalization, a child of the Industrial

Revolution, has certainly helped. It has shrunk human society and distance so more cultures have to communicate and find ways to integrate and collaborate. People are aware of disasters far from their homes, and actually work to alleviate suffering of people they will never meet. Governments support other nations when disaster hits. Climate change alleviation is a global affair.

The idea that cultures would become homogenized into a mass culture is proving to be wrong. Cultures are too complex and deeply rooted. People like being who they are.

At the same time, isolation can lead to chauvinism and blindness. A breath of fresh air from a different culture can revitalize individuals as well as a society. It doesn't weaken the home culture, it stirs in an interesting flavor into the cultural soup.

Beijing is taking advantage of its new role as an economic powerhouse. The 2008 Olympics and the 2010 Shanghai Expo not only put Beijing and China on the map, they have brought in global discourse. Both desperately needed. These fresh ideas themselves have given Beijingers new ways of taking on the challenge of a sustainable city.

China has embraced its global role of combating climate change, biodiversity, and other environmental crises. Beijing is experimenting with its own ideas about how to transport millions of people and resolve its air pollution debacle at the same time. So the welcome mat is out in front, and once they can embrace your new idea, they will add their Chinese characteristics and realities, to make it work for them.

What Beijing Has Done Towards Sustainability

Water is an enormous problem. The South North Water Transfer Project, is a monumental and controversial undertaking to bring the water of the Yangtze River up to Beijing. This is a testimony to how serious the problem of water is in Beijing.

So, water is expensive. The newer apartments have special water cards, for the different kinds of plumbing. Gray water, which can be used for toilets, is cheaper than water from the kitchen tap.

Air pollution is also a big problem. Desertification, encroaching from the Gobi Desert, is another. Air pollution from desert dust from the desert mixed with smog has serious effects on residents. Beijing Municipality has reduced the number of cars allowed in the city. It has vastly increased the number of subway lines. The bus network is incredibly intricate and affordable. It is designing a prototype bus so big that it can ride over traffic. It has also greened parks, highway intersections and divides, and planted trees on its mountain ranges to the north and west. The city is working on a lot of problems like these, systematically, looking towards 2020. Creating satellite cities, livable communities, and using resources sustainably, while at the same time, building the infrastructure that connects it all together.

There is also a migrant worker population that continues to grow in the city. This began in the '90s when villagers were brought in to build the new cityscape. Now many others have come in search of work. Urban professionals, originally here for university, prefer to stay as well.

Sustainability in this city? The Municipality and many of its citizens are aware of the problem.

There Is a Role Common People Can Play

There are many ways to help build a sustainable city. The city and the spirit and capacity of its citizens need to connect. People can help as individuals, as a family, or as an employee. People can think about how they'd like to contribute – to their local neighborhood or compound. This is a win-win activity.

Changes are already under way. The wisdom and culture of the past are again of interest to Beijingers. Not just by government policy but because people are looking for balance. Some are training in traditional Chinese medicine and acupuncture. Others are using Taiji and martial arts, and have developed these into exercise routines. Many, despite the lure of the ultra modern or television, still go out to the parks to enjoy ancient arts, sit outside in the parks or inside theaters if they have the means, and watch performances, dramas, calligraphy drawing as well as folk art.

Or, they are out doing modern ideas that have taken on a Chinese flavor. Ballroom dancing in the park, dancing as exercise, and country line dancing enthusiasts are out every weekend.

These are just some of the ways Beijingers take away the pressures of work, family and maintain their health. What is sustainability if not enjoyment of art? If not taking responsibility for your health? All art comes from the soil. All health comes from the soil too. There are many ways to maintain and deepen connections to the natural world. And to wake up.

I used to see many people out in the common areas at night and think, "Oh their apartments must be very hot." No, people also go out of their homes and socialize in the night. Kids bike and chase each other. Parents and the elderly with their young ones to teach them how to walk or how to bike. They want to be outside. Whether they are conscious of it, people are the living energy of a city.

There is, unfortunately a deep expectation that the government must solve these environmental problems. And a deep insecurity about the future. How can Beijing become a good place for families and future generations? We, the common people, we can choose to stand together.

Lu Xun, the great Chinese writer, woke up the Chinese people from their nightmare by writing so deeply to his people that their hearts were touched. He said that hope cannot be said to exist, nor can it be said not to exist. The earth had no roads to begin with but when many men pass one way, a road is created.

This is a satellite photo of Beijing. You can see the Western and Jundu mountain ranges that rim the western and northern boundaries of Beijing City. Population is 19,612,368 as of 2010. The metropolis has 14 urban and suburban districts and two rural counties.

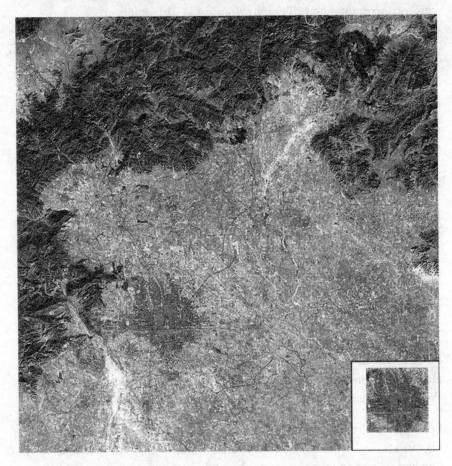

The inset shows the size of Beijing before 1990. Now the city covers the entire plain.

Navigating East/West Dialogue:
China and the U.S.

I hope this book begins a people-to-people dialogue, people and community dialogue and a people of Beijing to people in capital cities dialogue. And that the dialogue, like real dialogue does, leads to becoming, to being more.

We are after all the same species. We can evolve into a species noted for collaboration. We can create our own transformation into a species deeply conscious of the life on this planet and radiant with life.

What can we bring to the table of dialogue? First we need to notice our own blinders. Chinese do not want to be American. They like who they are.

I have found that people in Asia, east, south, north and west, who have been trading with China for centuries, can be very helpful. The right people, with very deep relationships with China, can give Americans perspectives we need. Asians can be good interpreters for us. People who help in this way are a kind of Everyhuman.

Each Everyhuman in this book has a story to tell. As the facilitator, I have tried to create a place where we can all get together and talk. I have assumed that you are someone unfamiliar with China or to Beijing. For this reason I start each chapter by describing how we met, something about them, interject explanations or provide background information here and there.

There is a glossary at the back. It contains some of the terms and people I have mentioned in the book. If you are already familiar, I apologize for explaining things you already know.

I am not a scholar of Chinese history, culture and modern society although I am deeply interested in such things. Nor am I professional in the field of sustainable development, although I have been living abroad and teaching global citizenship for many years. I am a teacher of dialogue.

What I have here is gleaned from my dialogues, both past and present. My experience at listening for what is not being said. My mistakes and blunders come from the blinders of my own assumptions. Or the blinders of Chinese people enveloped in part of their ethos that I cannot identify. Through deep and sometimes very painful experiences and at others joyful triumphs, I have awakened to the plain beneath my feet, thanks to my friends.

We are all babies at real dialogue but many of us are learning step by step the transformational power dialogue possesses. In the preparation of this book I used what was readily available from my collection of books on Asia, philosophy and on the Internet. I have developed gratitude for Wikipedia, a great source from which to start a journey. You are welcome to send me corrections. My intent always is to try and give some voice to what Chinese are thinking or unconsciously assuming, so they and their city come alive for you.

Implicit East & West

To do this as a gift, the problems of really understanding the other must be addressed again and again.

We don't belong to the same ethos. For example, all of Asia is very familiar with Confucius. Everyone in the West knows about God. You don't have to believe in Him or believe the same way but when someone says God you know which god is in the conversation, and when others infer or imply something about Him, you have a good idea what is being said.

In the West we know of Confucius but not much of what he actually taught.

We learn "spare the rod and spoil the child" perhaps, but nothing of the doors he opens so we can feel the heartbeat of nature.

When we both talk about home – the West has one idea in their head and the Chinese another.

I used to teach intercultural tourism English in Taipei at Wenhua University. When I pointed to anything historic, my students would say, "Oh, that place is very famous." "Why is it famous?" I would ask. Then they would be stuck – they knew in their heart why but they wouldn't know how to frame the answer so that I could grasp their feeling. They'd blurt out ideas and I learned to summarize them and repeat the story back. Yes, that is why it is so revered, they'd say.

Part of the problem was that they didn't think I'd would respect them if they told me something that Westerners don't think is "right." About the cave where a god lived, and why couples pray there. Why all this is real to them. Why they respect and value something passed down for generations.

That was my first introduction to the implicit issues in our two cultures, East and West. I discovered that people from Asia understood immediately about that cave and why it was so revered. I became interested in respecting their perspective. Diversity is great and we don't all have to think alike! We just need to create mutual respect.

Even Chinese who have been to the States and spent time there, may not know how to explain certain things. They may learn your culture but still not express theirs well. Americans need to realize that these Chinese were fighting the Cultural Revolution while we were watching movies, protesting the war, going to Vietnam or working towards the American dream. Even today, Chinese students rarely see movies. They are too busy studying.

Reading each other's literature or data is also problematic. Translators are people too, and they are also caught up in their own cultural context. That is why asking questions to make sure you understand is really helpful.

To understand these Everyhumans, even the ones who are American, it is important to try and think of them as human beings. Get below the culture stuff, both the ancient and the modern culture stuff. You will find if you read the same story twice you will understand the person better, for example. This is lieu of asking questions. To be curious is a great tool. Seeking to understand too.

For we are all in discovery mode now about each other as we head towards the same future. Understanding doesn't have much to do with knowing the language. Knowledge is helpful but not essential. Sometimes these can be barriers. I think listening deeply, trying to ask the right questions, leaving your mind open so you don't judge or assume too quickly – helps a lot. Beijingers like Americans a lot and are infinitely patient, and they really want you to understand them. It really helps if you feel the same way.

Acknowledgements

My great thanks to my editor, Li Shujuan, for her friendly support, even lending me her daughter Yan Ni as my intern when she realized I was desperately in need of getting going. Yan Ni, for her courage, care and resourcefulness. Guan Chang for good bridgework. My husband, Bob, for his eternal reinforcements. My teachers – my parents and master teacher Barbara Finklestein. My life mentor and cosmic humanist, Daisaku Ikeda. Tsunesaburo Makiguchi who taught me how to create the open space for dialogue. And so many wayfarers who, like me, have been on their own roads and have intersected with mine. Their points of light, and nightmares, have both turned into lanterns in the dark for me.

Mac Fan, the Everyman

Mac's and my relationship began in 1993. We met at an industrial park project between Beijing and Tianjin. The park needed a school and I was hired to encourage students from Beijing to attend. Mac was connected with the business of it all. We'd traveled there with the board members. I didn't realize it at the time – I'd been in Beijing just three months – but the project was in free fall, and the board meeting going on in the main office was just to hammer the nails into its coffin.

While Mac and I waited – for eight hours – for it to conclude, we talked. Eight hours is enough time to get to know someone. We talked about my dreams and his life, and by the end we had formed an idea together: a school where Chinese and learn to collaborate. We needed a way to change values that are taught in school so that Chinese and Americans understand how to work together better. His work at beverage and ramen companies were dead-ends, and I guess I listened deeply enough for him to realize that we came from the same place. We could grow my ideas about education on the fertile soil of a deep respect and readiness to work together towards something the world needed.

Mac Fan (third left, back row) with teachers and students at an NSCL practicum

We began to look for a new place for such an international school. Our commitment drove some of the same venture capitalists of the abandoned project to help us locate the right place. We ended up in Shangdi, a high-tech development zone in the northwest part of the city, which was just getting started. Its management was run by a wonderful man who let us have a building, fenced the grounds for us and would bring us music flutes and other goodies just to encourage us. Even though his own daughter was unable to attend.

Creating a school – any school – is not easy, and creating one with little capital but big ideas was even more difficult. We managed to overcome one difficulty after another. Mac and I would talk and then he'd turn to the person we were meeting with and talk and talk until the other person, the education bureau, businesses, or Shangdi management, whoever, really understood, and wanted to help.

At the New School of Collaborative Learning (NSCL) (1994-2004), through Mac, I learned more and more how to connect with how Chinese think. He learned through the doors I opened for him about the world but also about *junzi*, since no one in China really believes in such ideas anymore. Confucianism was discouraged then (no longer) but he began to take an interest. He taught himself how to excel at helping teachers and other staff, and then students. I came to rely on his judgment and trust his instincts and intuition. The students, in turn, deeply respected him.

He was able to explain modern China to me. He is a gift to foreigners like me because he is always forthright about how Chinese will think about something. He showed me the real way to make things happen. What matters and what doesn't matter at all. He helped me avoid many of the mistakes expats make.

This was our partnership. I handled the ideas of the school and he handled having the school there at all. I gave him an international platform to grow on, and he gave me a way to understand how collaboration could happen between China and the U.S. But he doesn't baby you. You have to also learn not to be so stupid.

I have chosen him for this book because I learned from him about what real friend-ship means, what really irritates Chinese people, and what is important to them. I became part of the fabric of Beijing. Instead of charging a foreigner through the nose for our first school building, we were charged $1 rent plus utilities for four years, until we were able to pay full rent. Chinese officials and friends supported us wholeheartedly at times at the cost of their reputation and even at times their lives.

When the school folded (this is another story) he was asked to be on the board of the Jane Goodall Institute in China and went to work on his country. He has never stopped. People now call him Fan Laoshi (Teacher Fan). He has helped countless wayward students, patiently led people towards making good food choices, and taken responsibility for his own self-development. He is a good example of the Even though the school is no more, today in our Earth Charter Communities Network there are several former teachers and staff, who we trained to teach so that you light up the hearts of your students and awaken their potential to save the world.

So we are now back, working on the same mission, and in our roles as partners. We are in a favorite coffee shop in Shangdi near his apartment, and our old school building is across Shangdi Circle. Of course we are having tea in tiny cups over a tea board. The staff knows us well and attend to us happily as we drink our tea and reminisce about the past and confront how to help the present. As usual, Mac wears blue pants and a wrinkled shirt, talks into his cellphone (a recycled one, of course) from time to time to confer with people about factory constructions in Hangzhou or with fellow Jane Goodall Institute (China) personnel.

His eyes brighten when he sees me and we begin.

*****

Mac Fan: I moved to a new apartment compound in 1995 after the first year at NSCL. We talked a lot about environmental issues at the school and slowly, walking back and forth from home to school, I began to notice the nature around me. I became aware of the new saplings, bushes, grass. I became aware that the landscaping, such as it was, was there just to attract new homeowners. I became aware of the crassness of the developers who cared only for nature's value to the property. Grass is not sustainable in this dry climate, but they used grass as much as possible because it looked good. I also began to get involved with my community association, to get support for the needs of owners as well practice the ideals of the school.

One of the central ideals of NSCL was that we all can, and need to, become more *junzi* – exemplary men and women in life. *Junzi* comes from the teachings of Confucius. To be *junzi* means that you do the right thing. We don't believe that we are capable of it. But if we just start, we become *junzi* little by little. A situation confronts you and you ask yourself what the right thing to do is. You decide to do the right thing no matter what the consequences.

When you start you will not always be sure what the right thing to do is. You will have to learn from your mistakes. If you keep trying, you will begin to sense what the right thing is before you do it. This helps a lot! You are creating the inner strength that is *junzi*.

Doing the right thing means doing the right thing for you and for others. The more you take such actions, the more you can transform your life. Time and space in the East is more flexible than in the West, perhaps because in the East, people knew they were interconnected with the rest of life. Certainly these past years this connection has diminished and most people feel becoming *junzi* is too difficult.

Stephanie: This "right thing to do" is similar to having the Right Stuff in the U.S. This "right" in the East though is more in tuned with a universal harmony. Confucianism is a philosophy whose premise is that man, nature and the universe are one.

"It is the characteristic of Heaven to be the Real. It is the characteristic of man to be coming-to-be-real. (For a man) to be real [i.e. to have achieved realness] is to hit the Mean without effort, to have it without thinking of it, entirely naturally to be centered in the Way." [1]

Mac: Not that we always did the right thing either. But we tried. And we learned through our mistakes. (*laughs*)

Before I was at NSCL, I had no belief in such things. I am the son of an engineer and a doctor originally from Zhejiang. We moved to Beijing in the 1950s and I was born here. During my formative years, I just studied a lot and got into good schools and in the end graduated from Renmin University and have an MBA from there.

But as the years went by at NSCL, I began to realize that there are good things about Chinese culture that I never realized, like *junzi*. I saw clearly that my countrymen were ignorant about these good things as well. We *did* have values that could matter in today's world. I began to study Confucius and Laozi and had my daughter study them as well. I realized that there is a qualitative difference between what Confucius said and how he is interpreted today. Nevertheless, I tried to do my best, every day, to be *junzi*. In this way during the years at NSCL I could at least try to be a good model. And after NSCL, it was a way to carry on NSCL in my heart.

At school we studied Lu Xun because he was such a great communicator. I liked him a lot in high school, so I read his work again. From a person of little hope in the world, I began to see a way forward. Not all of the time though. There are a lot of people, both here and in the West, who are doing really stupid things, so I am not always hopeful.

I deeply think collaboration between China and the U.S. is critical. I first went to L.A., was when we participated in a Model United Nations activity at Mission Viejo High School. I walked out of the airport and could feel freer. But that was in 1999. There are so many ways that the West has been hypocritical about China and so disrespectful. On the other hand, we Chinese are very complex. We are not easy to understand. But I have to say that we do have experience with growing great food that is healthy and delicious. But we listened to the West and have brought about our own stupidity. We know how to live a healthy life on the same land for thousands of years. You have learned to govern (or used to!) through the common people. We have a lot we have collaborate on!

Food Safety Guru

Mac: I began to experiment with growing my own vegetables. We lived on the 6th floor and had access to the roof. I began planting vegetables and didn't use chemical fertilizers or pesticides, so of course the insects ate all my plants. I learned through many failures like this.

I knew there was a problem with food safety. I was in the food industry for six years before becoming the co-founder of NSCL. I knew there were ingredients that those companies were putting into food products that were not good for people.

This problem got worse and worse. You couldn't go even a day without something in the newspaper. I saw then that the problem was widespread in China, and my own family was at risk. How could my family eat safely if the food in the supermarket and even the local vegetable markets was so unhealthy?

In 2002 I started looking for a way to buy good food in Beijing. At that time there were very few organic farms, and these were very far from Shangdi and very expensive. So I talked to friends and we started our own gardens – renting plots of land from farmers. For two to three years, every weekend, we would go there and take care of the farm. We grew vegetables, corn, wheat one year, and chickens. My wife, Liubo and daughter Yihan, went with me, and together we grew into a family very deeply engaged in making sure we ate well.

Our daughter definitely knows where food comes from, how to grow vegetables, feed chickens and get eggs. It was a very good foundation for her. She is now deciding at Duke University what kind of environmental work she wants to pursue. She has her own passion now.

Even in our garden, where we tried to produce good food, we had trouble getting to eat good food. We engaged a farmer to look after the gardens during the week and when we couldn't get up there on the weekends. The first year, even though we told them we didn't want to use any chemical fertilizers and pesticides, we discovered that he did in fact use them. When we asked him about it he told us not to worry, the pesticide had come from his farm so he was saving us this expense. Even farmers, who knew how to produce good healthy food, had been undermined by industrial agriculture

Food safety presentation in Kaifeng

Food safety presentation at Henan University

practices. Adding chemicals means less work for the farmer. So we learned to compost and add nutrients to the soil and taught the farmer, so we could grow and have the food the way we wanted it.

At a health and food seminar I attended in 2007 for the Jane Goodall Institute (China), someone suggested that I go to a Community Supported Agriculture (CSA) meeting. CSA is an international organization. I couldn't attend but my wife, Liubo, went and met the organizers of Little Donkey Farm and was very impressed.

We became members and buy our food from there. Usually we drive up each week to the farm, about 45 minutes from our home. I find the young people who manage the farm sincere and committed to doing a very difficult thing: respecting the farmers while at the same time offering a more sustainable way of producing food for Beijing residents. We established long-term relationships with these managers.

It was not easy for them to become successful, but they are. The farmers didn't trust them or believe them and neither did the consumers. Regular meetings with the farmers, workshops on why organic foods are better for your health with consumers, and letting co-op members rent their own plots of land and grow their own produce all helped.

Why? Because the co-op members created connections with the people who grow the food for their families. Over time, the consumers developed a trust for the products. Over time, the farmers saw the value of healthy and productive harvests. The Little Donkey Farm became a bridge, and community developed on both sides, and now the farmers and members have relationships as well. Farmers also help Beijingers with their plots of land. Members came to realize that paying a higher price for food enables farmers to give children a better education, and see the value of growing healthier food.

We buy less from supermarkets and more from organic farms we trust. Indeed, I believe we are part of the real economy, instead of being part of just stupid consumption. More and more people are realizing this.

Stephanie: So how do you become a smart consumer?

Mac: There are some ingredients we can't buy from farms we trust. So before we buy food at a store, we need to check the ingredients on the label carefully. Many interesting food additives – lots of them – are legal but actually harm us or are even dangerous. You can find out everything that goes in these products from the Internet or doing other research. It is just a matter of deciding to what extent you, the consumer, care about it.

That is why it is important to check the labels. Companies do not do long – term research and testing of their chemical additives before they add them to our food. Chemicals that were thought to be okay for decades are now found to be hazardous. They discovered the danger only because people became ill or died and experts traced it back to the chemicals. Who can guarantee the chemicals and additives that are put in today won't be found to be bad for people later? DDT is an example of this.

I think we have a good labeling system in China, and at least the producer puts in everything that is contained in the processed foods. "So they are honest!"*(laughing)*

We consumers should all try to use fewer chemicals ourselves. For example, detergents are really bad for our water and ecosystem. Try to minimize how much water containing these chemical detergents drains from your apartment. There are ways to do this. In our home, we reuse our gray water (water recycled from showers and washing machines) to wash our floors and toilets. Reduce waste – recycle as much as possible.

Water from plastic bottles is not healthy unless it is a Level 5 or 7, a marking that is on the bottom of the bottle. You need to make sure to see the BPA-free mark on it. Always try to reuse plastic bags and replace plastic bags with cloth ones as much as possible. Plastic is forever. It doesn't biodegrade. In my family, we just use metal thermoses.

Buying fewer things makes less waste. Buying what you don't need is a kind of greed, isn't it? It is not *junzi*. It is not the right thing to do. When you become greedy – buying more and more just because you desire it or because you can or because people around you have it – you lose the ability to see what is real and what is not. Greed clouds your thinking. I think this is what has happened to the people of China and around the world. It only took a few years to get this way. But we can decide to make a change and reconnect to the real world, to the real planet, and to real relationships. I want the real China to emerge from this stupidity. People can and will respect us then.

An educated consumer is the best customer is a start. But not just educated. They must be smart and proactive. Ask questions. Not just one. At least five. By the fifth question you can begin to tell whether an "organic" company is truly selling organic food. You can tell by the way they answer. Or by the answer itself. "Truly organic is impossible in China," is an example of a bad answer, because God's Green Garden and Little Donkey Farm prove them wrong.

When you buy clothes, gadgets, and supplies it is the same. Ask what they do to protect the environment. Ask them who made them. If any harmful chemicals are used. Within five questions, you can make a wise choice.

When buying food at the market, you can ask the same questions. When you buy food in cans or packages, read the labels. Ask people in the store questions about their products. Ask about the meat they sell. How they treat the animals, what they feed them. Educating yourself is the best way to go. Help yourself make wise choices. Buy cheap and be sick later or buy right and keep your health.

Stephanie: Is there a connection with NSCL here?

Mac: All this started, why I am so passionate, at NSCL. We did many activities that developed my own understanding about how to engage with people from the West. Our mission, to create self-motivated learners who want to be global citizens, was our task and through the struggle to live this mission, I learned how to connect my Chinese-ness with the rest of the world.

Inter-cultural collaboration was our method, but few of us knew what it meant or how to do it. No one was raised to be collaborative, after all. The main Earth Charter principle, to respect and care for the community of life, seemed to best describe our relationship to one another without having cultural differences get in the way. We didn't use a Western or an Eastern concept. We used the principles of the Earth Charter, which was created through dialogue, and designed to develop a just, peaceful and sustainable global community in tune with the rest of life. Not just my wisdom, your wisdom. Not just your wisdom, my wisdom. We designed the school culture on this basic premise.

We were a bilingual, bicultural international school. We had teacher teams – one Chinese, one foreign – in the elementary school classes. For junior high and high school we had teams of teachers teaching the different subjects – math, language arts, science, social studies. We had Chinese PE and art teachers. None of the Chinese had ever taught in an international school. None of the foreign staff had ever worked with Chinese staff as equals. We had never started a school before. So there were many, many problems, especially the first year. But we learned.

Nor was collaboration taught in schools here or in the West at the time. Sidwell Friends School helped us shape our concept and a curriculum, but at first teachers just taught according to how they were trained. My job, managing the affairs of the school, was to learn and think about the Western ways, and the unique ideas we ourselves added to the philosophical foundation. Then discover ways to teach collaboratively. You and I learned to collaborate and solve problems together. I then would think about it from my Chinese culture context and talk with the Chinese teachers. Using these experiences, I could also help the non-Chinese ones learn how to work together with the Chinese.

Creating a common culture at NSCL proved very helpful. For example, to demonstrate a sense of common ground between Americans and Chinese, every year we had our Valley Forge, Long March, March. Everyone was invited to reflect that it is not easy to start a country. Sometimes people have to suffer and struggle a lot. We'd gather all of the students (we were always very small) and march together behind a banner – an annual Valley Forge, Long March March banner – a certain distance. We'd then celebrate by eating George Washington's hoecakes and Chinese porridge (jiou). It became part of our NSCL culture. Not only was there reflection on the purpose of the march, there was also camaraderie – older students taking care of the younger ones – and besides, it was fun to march together. Doing these kinds of activities together created bonds. We recently had a reunion and many of us talked fondly about this activity.

New students would start a year at school disliking Chinese food, disparaging Chinese teachers, and sneering at Chinese history. But by the end of the year, through activities like these, and the culture we built, our insistence that equal respect be given to both teachers and between teachers and students, they soon learned to live the spirit of NSCL. The Chinese teachers learned how to communicate with more and more students, so by the end of the year, students had a real sense of China.

There were many times that Chinese teachers came to talk with me, and foreign ones came as well. I learned to understand foreigners better, to understand how to help them. I realized that their image of China is terribly distorted.

When we first started doing serious environmental education at NSCL, I didn't have a concept about what it was all about. We looked for a way to understand how to encourage environmental awareness. Our first attempt was with Xiyuan High School. We had them to our school and together created garbage containers for both of the schools. Then they asked us to their school and students presented papers about the environment in both languages.

This led me to consider environmental degradation from a Chinese point of view. We Chinese have been careful to reuse glassware – many, many Chinese reuse glass jars from instant coffee jars, for example. No one was rich enough to just throw things away that still could be used.

The government at the time urged the public to stop using plastic bags. There were many public notices about this on television and radio and at public places. What was the real point here? And what did all this have to do with me?

Then I got it. Thinking about the whole issue, I realized that the essential point was: make less waste. This was something everyone could do.

Chinese learn in school how to construct a way to logically examine some-

thing. They don't have creative writing but do learn to write compositions where they set down and develop ideas to their logical conclusions. But where does the logic come from? They learn, from their math, that to get to the right answer you need think in patterns, in formulas, so that all of the parts fit together. Only then you can see your way to the right answer. This polylinear thinking is one reason why we had both Chinese and American math at NSCL.

Mac: Make less waste was the beginning. From there we developed projects at school. We joined the Model United Nations program headed by the International School of Beijing, centering on their ECOWAS Environmental Program for our students. But soon we felt that such a global perspectives on the environment didn't help our students take action in their own lives.

So we created our own environmental forum program. Designed by teachers, these programs began with students studying the topic, say, water, and then researching environmental NGOs that are connected to the issue. Next they apply and interview for a job at an NGO they like. Finally, they study and prepare to debate the issue. We all learned from these forums by helping the process along.

This led to our great practicums. The practicums became part of the research that went into the annual topic. This fieldwork deepened the impact of the topic on all our lives. The use of drip agriculture in Shanxi taught me the value of water. I saw how deforestation causes the drought and sandstorms in Beijing.

I learned as I prepared these trips. I would connect with Chinese bureaucrats and to get their support. I developed an extraordinary relationship with a local bureaucrat in Shanxi. When we met in his office, I remember you saw the bed that he slept in when he had to work late at night. You stopped stereotyping our government officials. We all learned so much from these trips.

I sought out and built a relationship with CEPA (Chinese Environment Protection Agency) in Beijing. We had their experts come in to teach students about environmental problems. In 2002, our school provided the

U.S. Embassy Beijing, at its request, with a white paper on drought research we did with CEPA when the practicum was in Yanjing, just north of Beijing.

In 1998 Betsy Damon led the practicum and we went to Shandong Province where the Yellow River discharges into the sea. She taught us about the nature of water, why we must respect water. Water is life but we don't treat it with respect at all. Students realized water doesn't just come out of the tap. It is a very complex how the water gets there, and where it goes after it drains from our homes. How we treat it depends on what kind of future we will have.

All of these projects deepened my understanding but they couldn't have happened unless the Chinese in these areas opened up and were willing to talk with us. I helped teachers and students respect the officials and show that respect. Students considered their perspectives seriously, and teachers thanked them for helping our students think about the issues from the Chinese perspective. We did not act like ignorant and arrogant foreigners. People could tell the difference very quickly.

This was the product of countless hours of learning to collaborate at NSCL – students, parents, staff and teachers. Managing the affairs of the school, the grounds, transportation, building relationships with our landlords, between our bus drivers and the students, between the school and the education bureau taught me a lot. I learned how to get both the students to listen respectfully to Chinese people and the Chinese bureaucrats to want to provide this opportunity for our students.

So, learning to collaborate made me realize that I could help others collaborate with nature. This was the start of my commitment. The practicums became education for everyone. Our first practicum was to Chengdu to see the Living Water Garden and the pandas and village life at Wolong. I saw many beautiful things – water, mountains, so much beauty – this was the beginning. I saw in later practicums lots of garbage in beautiful places. It made me conclude that we have to do something to change how we are consuming. Otherwise, we will not have these splendid mountains and rivers anymore.

Later the practicums began to be designed by teachers who now outdid us with their ability to connect with experts who could teach our students more. One teacher began a relationship with Dr. Pan Wenshi and his Guangxi Chongzuo Reserve. Through his interest in her students, we created practicums for elementary students at the Reserve. Students began to thrive on the value of nature. This deeply impressed me.

It was at Guizhou that I first tasted really organic food – Chinese cabbage from the village in the mountain, cooked only with salt. It tasted so good and I realized what organic means. This was the beginning of my understanding about organic food.

Jane Goodall Institute, Harvest for Hope and Mission

Mac: I got involved with JGI around 2006 and was asked to be on the board. I was chairman from 2009-10 and tried to provide Chinese perspectives at the board meetings.

We have Roots & Shoots offices in Beijing, Shanghai, Chengdu and Nanchang. There are now more than 600 Roots & Shoots programs in China, from kindergartens all the way through university student groups, all of them implementing small-scale projects that show care and concern for the environment, for animals and for the human community.

The board tries to encourage students to create more and more projects by asking the questions they want answered. Such grassroots projects, which come from the students' daily lives, have a greater impact on their future.

There are more Roots & Shoots groups in schools every year. Figuring out the issues and trying to help. In Beijing alone there are 80 programs. The groups run the programs by themselves. Once a year we have a summit.

Since the program started in 1998, there have been many success stories – from organic gardens in schools to students who try to convince their school cafeteria to provide organic food. There are eco-family programs and eco-office programs – where they calculate footprints and ask people to change.

I also translated her book *Harvest for Hope* with my daughter. It showed me me how to construct a role for myself about food safety for the Chinese. I found I could explain her mindful eating idea very clearly and people began to seek me out. Not that any of what she says is secret, it is just that people, even people like me who are interested, don't know where to look. You can locate this information easily if you just look, is the lesson I learned from her.

The reason I decided to read the book in English was because I was stranded in Mongolia in a snowstorm for 5 days. I wasn't looking forward to having the same simple food every day and thought I would get very bored of it. But even though we had the same food every day, it tasted just right and was actually delicious – just as Jane described in her book.

The reason it was so tasty was because it was real local food, with no artificial colors, no artificial flavoring agent, and no thickeners. At the same time I was reading in Jane's book about all the different kinds of hormones and additives used in food, whether treated or radiated: eggs, chicken, milk, pork, beef, fish, shrimp, vegetable, fruit, corn, and so on. I realized that I could take this on as a mission.

In *Harvest for Hope* Jane Goodall gives readers easy access to the issues facing us about food choices, animal misery, and hazardous farming practices, and ways people can make simple changes. The same way she has done.

Mac Fan, and his daughter Yihan, with Jane Goodall

These are global issues of course. She reveals the hidden ways companies try and make a profit. Dairy problems, for example, where herbicides in feed remain in the milk and beef we eat. But also where fearless people have stood up against such people and won. All this led me to become passionate about letting my fellow Chinese know about this important book. So I translated it with my daughter. I am now painfully knowledgeable about such things. *(laughs)*

The reality is that it is our human dignity that is at stake here. Industry can be corrected by legislation and we can lend our verbal support to make sure it does.

But it is the individual's private consumption that needs to be checked as well. We need to value the dignity of our own life first and foremost. We need to protect ourselves now and we need to conserve for our future generations.

As she has said: Every individual matters. Every individual has a role to play. Every individual makes a difference. If every individual stops buying bottled water, the plastic pollution will be reduced dramatically.

It was through Jane Goodall that I learned about another truly organic farm, God's Green Garden. A mutual friend of Therese Zhang Zhimin, the owner of the farm, introduced Ms. Zhang to Jane. Jane wanted her story in the Chinese forward to *Harvest for Hope,* which was published in 2007.

I called her to find out more about her farm, and now we continue to meet and talk at Community Supported Agriculture (CSA) meetings. I visited her farm with my wife and discovered that her biodynamic farm truly is what she says it is. It is not easy to be solely responsible for a biodynamic farm, but she is doing it. From all my observations, I trust her practice and her products.

The 3-Egg Story

Mac: In 2008, while Jane visited Beijing, she stayed at the home of our board member Greg MacIsaac. My family had chickens that lay eggs on our farm, but for seasonal reasons, there were not many of them. Chickens have their own pace for laying eggs, but people in the egg business feed their chickens with hormones, so they will lay continually – but this is unnatural.

I knew Jane'd love to have a fresh and natural egg for breakfast. We do not feed our chickens any chemicals, so the output is not much. I managed to save three eggs for Jane. She stayed in Beijing for 3 days that year. I warned Greg that the eggs were for Jane only! *(laughs)* She really loved my story and of course enjoyed the eggs. We reached a deeper understanding because of these 3 eggs.

My Visit to Nanchang with Jane in 2008

Mac: I accompanied Jane to Nanchang to meet with Roots & Shoots groups and visit Poyang Lake together. We met with the local CEPA who showed us a video of the wetlands with all the migratory birds we were about to see.

The size of the lake has been severely reduced because of drought. We arrived at the wetlands. There were thousands of birds, of all kinds, foraging, talking and taking off occasionally. It was quite spectacular.

Jane stood in front, her hands on the back of her ears so she could listen to them. She suggested to the EPA officials to include the sounds of the birds in their new video instead of the human music that was there. It would make the video much more beautiful.

The birds were so fantastic and Jane was deeply trying to listen to them. But the students were talking loudly to each other, so she couldn't hear well. Jane turned back, calmly but in her inimitable way spoke sharply with them because they were not taking advantage of being with the birds. Jane, who has lived in jungles and respects the communication that can go on between humans and animals in the wild, was trying to make the point that we all need to try harder to be connect with life.

To me, that showed that Jane is a person who is *junzi*. It is a rare opportunity to meet such a person. The Roots & Shoots students needed to be reminded that here was an opportunity to connect with nature and learn something vital to their future.

Stephanie: How is Make Less Waste connected with Beijing's Development as a Sustainable City?

Mac: One of the biggest issues in Beijing is what to do with so much waste. For now they are putting waste in dumps around the city and it smells very bad. The dumps are full and no one wants to have one near them. There is no way to hide the garbage. They cannot burn it because it is mixed and has plastic and chemicals. You know the Germans are still burning theirs and now reports of cancers are surfacing there. That is why it's better not to create waste to begin with.

Our youth league has been criticizing the city for not finding better ways to educate city residents on how to do this. There are recycled bins and plastic bags for separating the different kinds of garbage – but still people are not doing it and are unaware of its importance.

The government is trying but it needs to make sure that this subject is brought up every day. Public education should be set up so everyone is becomes much more aware and takes action. Talk it up in the news, on the radio, on CCTV – they have lots of ways to do this. Let people know where their garbage goes. Trace it to the garbage dump and go there and interview people and have a daily update on the level of smell.

We have such a dump up here near Shangdi. In the Environmental Park! Officials have to ask the people who work at the dump, to cover it when important people come. It smells that bad. It is a nightmare. Those poor people in the neighborhood cannot open the windows on hot days.

This is the business of everyone but people don't realize it. So we need to make Beijing more conscious. Have everyone talk about it. Then people will find the best way.

Like for kitchen waste, for example. I think all the apartment compounds should process it locally. Make compost for the landscaping and gardens on the balconies. There are ways to do this without it smelling. Earthworms and such. The resident gardeners could be retrained to do this. The technology is already available for this.

Reducing the footprint of kitchen waste would be the simplest way to address the problem. Keeping it in the same apartment compound reduces the amount that has to be transported. We wouldn't need to have so many workers in a thankless jobs and would need fewer dumps.

Why should we have a city utility that no one wants, likes to be near, or hates to work at? My idea won't just help the planet, it will reduce the financial cost of such a bad removal system. Every day these trucks are removing tons of garbage from all of our apartments and compounds. Think of it.

Many migrant workers today also pick up waste, but this is not an answer either, because the work is menial. This is not a meaningful way to make a living. This is not the right way – picking up recyclable waste like plastic bottles. The bottle manufacturers should stop making them. If there are no more meaningless jobs, workers will feel they can provide for their families and also will want to be helpful to their society and the environment.

I have to say though, that Beijing has changed a lot in the last 10 years and in another 10 it will change even more. People will feel ashamed that they were so irresponsible. Better to comply and take care of your garbage today, conscientiously, rather than be fined and shamed later. Beijing could become a model. China is already handing out fines for equipment and furniture that is covered in plastic, like sofas. Unfortunately, people have to realize that *they* themselves have to change.

I think the world should follow the lead of the Chinese people and do what we have been doing for thousands of years – drink a lot of boiled water. Such water is safe.

How can we scale down the purchases of unsustainable goods so we can live in a sustainable city with a healthy economy? Basically there is no solution. *(sighs gloomily then laughs - Chinese laugh at hopeless situations.)*

Stephanie: Hope can make a road, Lu Xun says.

Mac: The only solution is self-awareness – educate yourself. There are websites and many ways to learn about farming and food processing methods today. Make use of them. Our government cannot forbid plastic after all. But you can change your habits anytime you want. All this information is accessible. It is a matter of care and seriousness. Do people really care about what they eat themselves and feed to their children?

The Chinese government is already concerned about obesity here. The next 10 years will be no dream. Living wisely will be very hard. It'll be like a soccer game when you have fewer people than the other team. People aren't going to be looking to go on the offense – they are just going to try and defend their lives.

This – the awareness of the dignity of our lives – must be the basic principle for our time, on which all of our actions rest. Limit consumption of physical materials means purchase only what adds to your wellbeing and that of others. Make use of our physical bodies – which is energy – for our own sakes and to help others.

What we need is a deep change of heart. A restart – so we can tackle, in a real way, the problem of feeding 1.3 billion people and then help others to do the same with their populations. We can all become *junzi* after all.

Little Donkey Farm,
Creating Farm to Fork, Step by Step

Little Donkey Farm is the culmination of a century of ideas and effort passed from one generation to another to help the villagers of China climb out of poverty.

These young people who run Little Donkey Farm are the disciples of agricultural experts who, from the beginning of the 20th century, have been on a mission. First they want to connect the farmer to modern society. They also want to forge a better relationship between rural villages and the city made worse by postmodern degradation of the soil. Finally they want to rebuild the human connection, and agriculture's connection, to nature that agribusiness has destroyed through avarice and thoughtlessness.

For centuries local farmers provided food for this city. Educated from the traditions of Chinese philosophy but illiterate, they evolved in a way that was not separate from the gentry, merchants and traders, and soldiers within the city, but was certainly distinct.

The various changes of dynastic rule never changed the basic role of the farmer, which was to provide for the people in the city. However, the city got larger and larger. More and more water and land had to be diverted to feed the people. Major floods and river changes especially during the Qing Dynasty, made it more difficult to meet growing demands.

Only in the 20th century was there an effort to help peasants. With the establishment of the PRC, more change occurred. Mao Zedong, son of a farmer himself, knew how much he owed the peasants. He instituted universal public education, created communes and infrastructure, and sent youth to help the farmers at harvest time. But the culture of the village and that of the city was by this time so different, that even well-intentioned efforts failed to gain much headway.

Liang Shuming(梁漱溟) and James Yen (Yen Yangchu 晏阳初), both educated abroad, were the pioneers of the early rural reconstruction efforts in the 20s. They built institutes and carried out research as well as worked with farmers. Through experiments and study, new approaches were implemented, but change was slow in coming. The commune brought modernization but not much benefit to individual farmers. In the 1990s, under Wen Tiejun from Renmin University, a new reconstruction era began, this time centered on helping farmers overcome the additional damage caused by consumerism and the market economy. In 2002 a Yen Yangchu Rural Reconstruction Institute was created in Zhaicheng Village, in Ding County of Hebei to work on this new reform attempt. There they developed two areas of work – development of a farmers' cooperative and ecological housing.

This is the story of the effect of that institute on the management of Little Donkey Farm. These young activists have worked hard, have gone through a lot, and have sacrificed a lot, but revel in their experience. Living life for them means working with farmers and doing research at Zhaicheng. In 2007 they moved their operations closer to Beijing and closed the institute in Hebei. Little Donkey Farm began operations in 2008. They are, and have their eyes on, the future.

Little Donkey Farm is a success because these young people have learned how to be a bridge.

But this bridgework is beset by still more problems. The needs of the growing metropolis they serve and the desire of its citizens to eat and live well is juxtaposed with the pressure to sell the land to create developments. This new wealth brings additional problems for farmers and their families.

Little Donkey Farm is a success, a success that comes from the bonds of a common experience. These young activists may be at Little Donkey Farm now, but the years at Zhaicheng are what binds them together and stirs their souls. It is who they are, and why they work with the city residents and why they have the support of the farmers. How will they weave the next Zhaicheng in their lives?

I first went to Little Donkey Farm (LDF) with my graduate students to show them what global citizens did. It was the first time they saw an organic farm. It was very cold, December, so the farm was at rest. The main room was full of people picking up the seasonally stored winter foods like Chinese cabbage, white radishes and such. Actually, they were picking up the food for their fellow members as well. The work area was loaded with produce. They also have a shop with dry goods like rice and beans, handicrafts and preserves from the different farms from all over China, ones who have been trained at Little Donkey Farm, or which LDF feels confident enough about their quality.

Ms. Shi Yan, spokesperson for Little Donkey Farm, showed us around the farm. My students were deeply impressed and inspired to see for real what we had talked about all semester. Animals treated decently. Delicious food. Care of the soil. Mindful stewardship of the land.

Shi Yan was not present at the following interview. She is a doctoral student of Dr. Wen. She spent six months on a CSA farm in the United States in 2008 and came back with an awakened understanding of how to have a biodynamic farm. She connected Little Donkey Farm to the international CSA movement. She is normally the face of this enterprise but I wanted to look deeper into what makes Little Donkey Farm tick. I was invited to interview the management as a single voice.

They have a unique collaborative management system that evolved along with their partnership. A harmony through diversity. Each voice adds something to the bond and something to the wisdom and something to the joy that comes from their heartfelt lives.

When I first interviewed them, we sat in a circle outside of the main building. It took a while for me to grasp what was really distinctive about this group. Through further research and contemplation, I realized that I was with extraordinary people who together are creating the future for both the rural villager and the Beijing resident. I feel honored that they took the time to help me understand the now.

*****

The Mission of Little Donkey Farm

We respect nature, promote ecological agriculture, and hope that this relationship of mutual trust can be established between people, will promote positive urban-rural interactions, a harmonious society and a sustainable environment.

Yan Xiaohui:
General Manager

Yan Xiaohui: I am the general manager and in charge of distribution. Huang Zhiyou here (*gestures to the man on my left*) is in charge of public relations, administration and biweekly newsletters. Yuan Qinghua's (*gestures to his left*) concern is to ensure that the seeds for our farm are organic. He has a degree in bio-agriculture so this is how he supports. Shi Yan, a Renmin University doctoral student of Dr. Wen, does public relations and research. Lao Liu (*indicates the man to my right*) here has always worked with the farmers, both in Zhaicheng and now.

We work together well because we were all in Zhaicheng. We were there to help the farmers. But the farmers did not trust us. The farmers could not fathom that a bio-agricultural farm was valuable. They saw us let the weeds grow sky-high. We sorted garbage for composting. We did agricultural experiments. Nevertheless, the point of the institute was to help the farmers.

We have made some headway. We have helped farmers develop cooperatives, showed them how to buy coal and other material in bulk so they could pay less for it. They rarely believed us back then.

These challenges created a bond. We didn't have much income. Our families and girlfriends pressured us to be like other people. To find a good income and work towards getting a house and a car. Build our fortune so we could marry. Consumers and academics asked us why they should buy organic food? How can you prove that this is organic? Experts told us that China needs industry to feed so many people. But we continued to work at what we believed was right in our hearts.

When we knew the institute in Zhaicheng was going to close, we created a plan, together with Dr. Wen. We began to look for a place to have a farm that could be bio-agricultural. Little Donkey Farm came to fruition in 2008.

Yuan Qinghua's expertise was critical. We had problems when the farm was being set up. The company that owned the land wanted a more business-as-usual farm. But Yuan patiently explained our way of farming to them and why it was so important. Through our cooperative efforts, we also obtained the support of Haidian District. Through these kinds of experiences, we learned to work as a team and not give up until a problem was solved. We didn't have any business experience, so I went south and worked in companies to learn business practices for two years.

Stephanie: I understand Little Donkey Farm is now supported by Haidian and the Chinese People's University of Agriculture and Rural Development

Institute. The Beijing Hongda Brilliant Investment (Group) Co., Ltd. also helped build this research base, right?

Yan: Yes. Once we had the farm, the forming of the cooperative was next. In 2007 before we moved to Beijing, people would come all the way from Beijing to buy our products in Zhaicheng in Hebei Province, which was quite a distance. Now we wanted them to support our goals by providing steady support for our organic products.

The next step is an example of our commitment to our goals — to what we want to do together. We first helped consumers form cooperatives in Beijing. Then we set up our own co-op in 2009. People put in shares. Shi Yan connected us with CSA. I returned in 2009 and the Little Donkey Farm became operational.

Little Donkey Farm is also a training center, like the institute. We have two training programs that we charge money for every year and many others that we do for free. We also set up our bioagricultural system here, so we can show farmers how to find ways to go back to traditional farming methods or consider the organic market for themselves. We have had many trainees and local farmers help us farm. Our 10 programs train about a 1,000 farmers a year. They come from all over China.

At the same time we educate members and Beijing residents how to eat wisely, how to grow healthy food, and we supply them with a food basket every week.

Huang Zhiyou:
Membership

Huang Zhiyou: I came to Dr. Wen's institute in Zhaicheng in 2004. I love walking just with my bare feet. I used to sort garbage for composting back then, and everyone was concerned about me. But I love to feel the ground underneath my feet. I came to the institute because I heard about the radical environmentalist James Yen, loved all life, even pests, and believed everything in nature has a right to exist. We need to safeguard that right. Even if you have to quarrel with colleagues to protect weeds, for example. This is reasonable, I believe.

I am from Shaanxi Province and was born in 1982. I went to Northwestern Agricultural University and graduated in 2000. I always wanted to farm but my family didn't want this. They would lose face if I did. So I went to another province and worked on a farm there. I love Gandhi, poems, nature. I also taught myself Traditional Chinese Medicine.

I wanted to lead a life that was part of nature. In 2003 I read about this institute in the countryside of Hebei. I knew this was the kind of life for me.

I arrived in March 2004 when the sandstorms were very strong. The institute was a little deserted but I liked it. I was the first university student to sign up.

I began by sorting garbage and making it into fertilizer to enrich the soil. This was is my first responsibility. I felt lucky because I had followed my gut. And because I did, I was able to be here at the beginning. This life fits my personality.

In Beijing there are too many houses and too many people and it is too crowded. Because of my work, I know the value of discarded waste. So, I can't bear to mix my peels with other garbage like people do all the time in Beijing.

The peels can be buried under trees. As they decompose they will become fertilizer for the trees. But people just throw them away in garbage cans with other garbage.

It is so dirty and so smelly. Think about the old men and women who search the garbage for something to sell – you can see it is really inhumane. So when I am in Beijing I try my best not to eat fruit.[1]

Yan: You see why Huang Zhiyou is now in charge of membership relations. Once members sign up, he helps them understand what is important to nature. Huang knows how to communicate these kinds of habit challenges. To learn how to eat seasonally and to recognize its benefits. To explain why vegetables don't look so nice, compared with ones that have pesticides. Why they are not as big. That some have worms occasionally, etc, etc.

We encourage seasonal eating because it fits with the rhythm of the planet. It also means that we eat more of the same vegetables and for a longer time. Huang create recipes for members. He also puts them in our magazine.

He also helps with farmland transition. Preparing the soil, detoxifying it, and nurturing it back to health is a vital part of our work of course.

Yuan Qinghua: We all started by doing farm work. We are part of the original group of students and volunteers in Zhaicheng. The first thing we did was try and make friends with the farmers. Dr. Wen encouraged us to build upon the past and added three fundamental principles to guide us:

Yuan Qinghua:
Bio-agriculturalist

- Provide free training for the farmer;
- Create and strengthen the working cooperatives;
- Raise the level of income for farmers.

The structure of the village is quite different from life in the city. The most important thing in the village is your relationship with others, how you feel about somebody. Next to be considered are basic principles for living wisely. Only after these is the law considered.

In modern society the first thing is the law. So you can see why there is such a gap. We do not focus on the law with them. Only on establishing good relationships. In the village if you have the right relationship, then anything can be done.

We try and raise the level of the cooperatives through community building – education, culture, environment, and the health of elders. So we provide training.

Yan: We were all just volunteers at the institute. There was no structure. As we evolved, people demonstrated different interests and abilities. We didn't have elections or appointments. We just evolved into this management system.

We like this structure. Other CSAs are not like us – they are more like normal co-ops. We are different.

Little Donkey Farm is a go-between. No one tells the farmer what to do. It takes a long time to know what the right thing to do is when everything is integrated into this bridge-building.

Their interest is how to develop, which to them means make more money. But our goal is to help the farmers build sustainable development for themselves by raising organic products for others. It is our job to help the farmers understand that this is the best way for them as well.

Their children, the young people, have already left to work downtown in the city. That is a loss to nature, to a sustainable living for their children, and at the same time a loss of healthy food for the city residents. We have to show them that they can be successful at farming and earn enough for their families.

Stephanie: How do you work with the farmers then?

Yan: First, we try and build our targets together. Second, together we plan how to operationalize and construct the target. Third, and this is the most important – culture construction with one another.

For this we use Dr. Wen's 3Ps: people's livelihood, people's unity, respect for other people's culture. Wen crystalized these points from extensive research in China as well as abroad.

Yuan: I work a lot with the farmers. When we have meetings, when and where is a big problem. The concept of time is different. You cannot say 6:30. You can only say "after lunch" or "after dinner," things like that. Of course, we also have different ideas about when we have dinner. Where is also a big problem. Someone may like or dislike someone else and so we can't meet there.

There are lots of things you need to consider beforehand before you meet with farmers. They are not going to be well organized. It is just going to be about what they think is right. We then get their points correctly, summarize them, create collaboration and act together. My experience with meetings includes: No one shows up, no one wants to talk, and things like that. No result is another. A lot of homework needs to be done before and after the meeting. Then you can solve problems.

They have their feelings, their histories, and generational problems. And despite these problems, you have to find ways to build the relationship.

How I Developed My Relationships with Farmers

 This story starts when I was at university. I joined a student group wanting to help Chinese agriculture. During my sophomore year, together with other students in the group, I collected clothes for impoverished villages. We were surprised that we could collect so many. The problem was we didn't know where to transport them. We contacted a village's public relations department, and the local council offered to help transport the clothes to the village.

On April 17, 2003, a car sent by the council came and picked us up. Before we left, we prepared food and water for ourselves because we knew the conditions in the village were poor, and we didn't want to bother the villagers.

After we arrived however, a feast was prepared especially for us, including cooked chicken and wine, because the local council had informed villagers so they could welcome us.

In such impoverished villages, chicken and wine are very precious, and only eaten on festivals or at ceremonies when the farmers will cook and drink together.

Although I and other students were very moved by the villagers' enthusiasm, we were not happy because we had bothered them despite all our efforts not to do so. After that, we didn't go through the local government.

The next year, I heard that there was a girls school where students from impoverished families could be trained as nannies. We decided to transport our clothes there.

This time the school welcomed us simply, which made us comfortable. I told the girls why my student group tried to help. Then the girls started to tell their own stories: Someone lost her parents, another's family member got sick or hurt in car accident, a mother killed her husband because of domestic violence, etc.

When the girls told the stories, they started crying, and finally everyone was crying, including me. Again, my group was not happy because we'd opened their wounds. This was unfair to the girls because they were already suffering from a tough life. Before we left, the girls sang the song "Gratitude" to thank us. Every time I remember this song, I feel sorry for those girls.

Then I knew I had to do something more useful. I found it at the Yen Yanchu Rural Construction Institute in 2004.

I first went to the institute for my sociology field study. I stayed after I graduated in 2005. I was so excited because I could finally devote myself to my work at the institute. What surprised me was when I began work, the first job they gave me was to transport dairy manure!

I thought I would be working with farmers on using manure in their fields. I had planned to devote myself to building homes for the village and do research on farming. I felt a little disappointed that now I had to actually get my hands dirty. I drove a tractor and dumped manure from the cows every day. I had a bad smell about me that wouldn't wash away. It was with me wherever I went, even in the dining room and the dormitory.

It was the beginning of all kinds of happiness and pain that occurred throughout the process of creating the cooperative.

I argued with everyone. Whether we should keep our donkey, whether we should build a house, whether our organic agriculture matches the farmers' needs, whether there is a connection between my work and village buildings, etc. There was always much confusion and regret between my dream and the facts.

But I loved to do experiments using my knowledge of biology with the help of an expert who worked as a volunteer. I learned about the microorganisms in manure. I learned that the fertilizer and chemicals used widely in farming poisons the producer, the soil, as well as the consumer. I then designed ways to combat the poisons and revitalize the soil.

I tried to show farmers how to apply my new techniques. I thought if farmers could use these techniques, they'd save a lot of money because chemical fertilizer is very expensive. It would also reduce the health damage to themselves and other. However, I only had a minor effect on local farming even though we demonstrated the effectiveness of my work. Then I had to stop all experiments because the institute closed.

When we established the farmers' cooperative in Zhaicheng, I participated in every activity. I went to the co-op almost every evening. After learning and discussing farming techniques and principles, farmers and I would play games, appreciate music together, and sing together. Everybody had fun. However my trainees wouldn't learn on their own initiative. So I told them "I won't come tomorrow, and you have to manage it by yourselves." The next day, I'd show up 30 minutes late on purpose, and saw all of them doing nothing but sitting and waiting for me. At the end of that first day, I'd say, "I really won't come tomorrow because I have to go back to the institute. You must manage it by yourselves!" But I heard that the next day the trainees still did nothing and then just went home after a while.

I was upset a lot because if the farmers wouldn't learn, my work at the cooperative would be in vain. I'd try then to remember Dr. Wen Tiejun's words: "The biggest failure is when farmers don't accept what we think is right."

Between 2005 and 2006, Qiu Jiansheng left for Hainan, and I had to take on more work at the institute office. I needed to prepare for training, launder the sheets, do accounts, document financial information, and manage office supplies. Although this kind of work was mind-numbing, I could bear all kinds of work except training at the Zhaicheng farmers' cooperative. I was too angry with everyone there.

During Spring Festival in 2006, I still argued a lot with everyone. However, things changed in the cooperative. Before farmers proposed things that were not feasible. But now the council focused, on a feasible program of growing sweet potatoes. After a series of market investigations, we decided to plant organic sweet potatoes on one mu of land.

This is when I found out that for farmers, your relationship is the most important thing. The council organized a meeting every five days. The most punctual people were my students or my colleagues' students. They came on time and showed up most of the time because they had learned something from our training, and we had built a good relationship with them. It hadn't occurred to me that the relationship-building I did back then would pay off. But it had an obvious influence. After that I went to Zhaicheng village more, and had dinner with villagers often.

A good relationship always brings more than you expect. The leaders of the cooperative and I did most of the steps for planting of organic sweet potatoes. But there were always a couple of regular members who joined in. The most impressive result was that we had about 40 members help transplant the seedlings in the rain. I was moved and I had more confidence in them.

Everyone changed, including me. Members no longer relied on me. They had a clearer mind. The relationship between the farmers and us was much better. I believe our intention to search for the right way to reach out to farmers was achieved through our resolve and perseverance.[2]

Stephanie: So you have broken through?

Yan: It is Western logic to think there is a breakthrough. This is a work in progress.

With the market economy now here in China, it is even harder to build this relationship. But we are doing a much better job now because the consumer is not that far away. Little Donkey Farm is the bridge between the two.

Stephanie: Tell me about your consumer cooperative.

Yan: There are different kinds of memberships. A general membership has two seasonal fees. Season One is from spring to summer and Season

Two is from autumn to winter. Each week members get a box of vegetables. They don't have a choice of vegetables, unless they really dislike something. Eggs and meat are a separate order, but you need to have a box of vegetables to have the right to order this because we don't have enough meat and eggs.

Some Beijinger co-op members help each other by rotating who goes and gets the vegetables in a neighborhood. We also deliver to certain areas and members pick up their boxes from these drop-off points. Some come out and get their produce for themselves.

Then we have working share members who rent plots of land. You can rent and farm all by yourself or you can engage a farmer to help you. We have 20 who farm and another 20 who engage farmers.

We have regular meetings for all members three times a year. At these meetings, we bring up certain issues we feel important to mention, and provide news. Then everyone participates in the discussion. There is a second part where members can talk together, solve problems and discuss matters of interest to them.

We have lots of meetings with the farmers. Almost every day and then three times a year we have big meetings and have dinner or lunch together. This is when we do the targets.

We have 700 customers, and 40 working share members. We hire their help from the villagers. Mostly older people. At first the villagers and farmers thought we were crazy to farm without using pesticides. Then they discovered that even without pesticides there is a good harvest. After that they started to enjoy it. This is the way we create change.

Stephanie: What is your message?

Yan: Organic agriculture is a communication, a dialogue where everybody can chat and in this way come up with new ideas. We didn't start with the aim to provide the city with more green food. It was to make the people who live on the land, live better.

In fact we don't really need a donkey. We have a tractor and electric grinders, so there is no need for us to use a donkey. We can keep a dog for fun, but why keep the donkey? We argued about this and the donkey stayed.

If we compare the big farm in the U.S. with the little family farm here in China, the U.S. has many advantages. Too many to talk about. But at high cost and low efficiency.

Coal can only be used for another 120 years and fossil fuel for 40 years. What do we do after that? We don't have to wait to stop using it because the price of oil is already rising and soon we will not be able to afford it. So this is the issue: Can we still develop using less energy or using no energy at all?

We at Little Donkey Farm want to find our own sustaining lifestyle and find a way for Chinese agriculture to exist forever as well. We must find and use our own inner wisdom to produce continuously and sustainably forever. Our production and society must become sustainable. A sustaining agriculture is forever.

To do this we must work. We must have passion if we are going to achieve our goal. Passion from beginning to end.

The process of communication is the process of making progress together. This too is sustainable development. If I can inspire you, this is progress. The process of communication is the process of continuing to think and improve ourselves, as quickly as possible. We must value the things in our minds. Maybe one word from a person in a certain circumstance can lead you onto a new road. Especially at our age, some inspirations can change us and help us to find our way.[3]

Stephanie: Has your cooperative developed? What's next?

Yan: I think it is more that the society has progressed. The environment is changing. The Chinese people are more concerned about their health. About what they are eating. We are at the right place and time. Farmers do get more income from using organic methods. We can pay them more because the co-op member pays more. Like I've said, we are a bridge.

We built on all those bloody accidents like the milk disaster of 2004 (*tainted milk has continued to cause the death of many babies and injure many more).* These people paid the price, but now the scandals have forced others to wake up. The level of knowledge is higher and Beijingers are better informed. The Beijing consumers lead the nation, so it is very important to educate them.

Right now, we don't need more people to join, because we can't grow any more on this plot of land. But we want to attract more and more customers. We are looking at other places around the city. Diversity will make our program stronger and bigger. It is hard to say when. Over the next five years, because there is no guarantee how long we can use this land.

We have other problems. Big companies are copying some of our methods, but they do a lot of fake things too, so this is not good. There is still plenty of fake organic and green washing. And these companies don't have the goal of helping farmers. They are businesses. We can help more people if we expand.

We also want to train more and more people from all over China. Even more than we do now.

We have a delicious lunch and then I see they are washing the dishes with something, not detergent.

Yan: We use wheat chaff to wash dishes. It does a good job of taking away all of the oil and food.

Stephanie: Where can people get wheat chaff??

Yan: Forget it. It is more expensive. The chaff costs about 70-80 yuan per jin (500 grams) and regular detergent only costs 1.6 yuan. We do it because it is a step. The more we can find ways to show people how to make small steps, the more people will.

By the way, many of the farmers around here are now rich. They are millionaires because they have sold their land-use to companies or the government for urban development. So now we and they have other problems.

Stephanie: After learning so much from Liang Shuming, James Yen and Dr.

Wen these 10 years, now you have more consumers and more land, do you have some new ideas you want to pursue?

Yan: Yes. We want to go back to some of the traditional methods. Yen and Liang brought modernity to farmers, but now we are trying to go back to traditional ways. There is a book, *Farmers of Forty Centuries or Permanent Agriculture in China, Korea and Japan,* by the American F. H. King, D.Sc. He came here a hundred years ago in 1909 and was shocked by the great farming going on in China. Americans ignored him but several years ago, some Chinese rediscovered the book and have translated it into Chinese. (*laughs at the irony*) We've lost a lot of these methods. But now we are reading the translation and discussing this.

American agronomist F.H. King toured China, Korea and Japan, studying traditional fertilization, tillage and general farming practices. His book was published in 1911, by his wife, Carrie Baker King, shortly after his death. He lived before agribusiness practices and was profoundly interested in how to farm the same soil and renew it sustainably. He studied agricultural practices of ancient cultures. His book has become an important organic and biodynamic farming reference.

Stephanie: Why are you so interested in the traditional?

Yan: Organic – biodynamic farming – is traditional farming. It has a long history and we used to have lots of experience. It is meaningful to find out what will work now. For example, eating seasonally. Eating only local vegetables. Before we became part of modern society, we just had cabbage and such every day, but that was just the way it was back then.

We can design different ways of eating cabbage – pickled or preserved – but what you should have is... cabbage. This is the direction we are going.

Looking at China before, since Peking Man, people ate the nature around them. Human beings observed nature. Nature competes, but also is in harmony. There is a certain rhythm, like our calendar, which creates rhythms for farming. This is sustainable, this is living in harmony.

We are also trying some micro-finance, because the situation is very hard now for farmers, so we are also checking into this. The real stories about the farmers who are now rich? There are many sad ones – killing other people, killing themselves. Lots of these stories. Peking Man instead of realizing the dream of an awakened rural consciousness as Liang Shuming hoped would happen.

The Chinese Village and the Development of Peking Man

The village has had a long history of abuse. The Tang Dynasty attempted to nationalize the land. The main tax burden, especially corvée labor, was borne by the free peasantry on a per capita basis. The government had to keep as many peasants as freemen as possible, so it could collect taxes. In 485 they established an "equal field" system in which all healthy adult peasants were assigned land of specified dimensions. Joint holdings of a couple amounted to 140 mu, or nineteen acres. Some part of this land could be held as crop lands for mulberry trees, and other kinds of orchards. The rest was returned to the government upon death.

This stabilized the financial foundation of the central government. The "three-chiefs system," was created to enforce this complicated landholding system, and bring in the taxes. The people were divided into groups and mutually responsibile for one another's conduct and tax payments. Five families made a neighborhood, five neighborhoods a village, and five villages an association. Each type had a chief, hence the name. Such collective-guarantee systems, which existed in the ancient past, continued more or less up to the present.[4]

In the 1920s James Yen experimented in Ding Xian and Liang Shuming school set up a school at Zouping, Shandong. They were only the earliest and most prominent of hundreds of village projects, educational foundations, and government zones which aimed to change the Chinese countryside. After 1931 there was an attempt to build the village economy, culture, and political structure, including pioneering work in village health.

Being a Peasant in New China

These efforts connected the peasants to the overall changing political scene. These peasants were the heart of the Chinese Revolution and to a large extent, gave the victory to Mao Zedong and the Communist Party over the

Nationalists and Chiang Kai Shek. For these reasons, helping the peasants better themselves and enable the village to shake off the past and join the modernization going on in China, was a high priority in the minds of the PRC.

Throughout Chinese history, though there were many peasant revolts, land issues didn't change much. In 1949, however, The Outline of the Land Law of China act redistributed areas in the north of China and in Shandong and Jiangsu provinces. Fanshen, meaning to 'turn the body,' meant to enter a new reality in the post-land-reform era, and millions of peasants saw their lives change. They were able to own their land, to learn to read, women now had rights, and villages could elect officials. By 1953, 300 million farmers had come into their own.[5]

However, the farmers were left somewhat leadership-less at first and so grew what they liked. Farming means irrigation and irrigation needs communal effort. Eventually, they began to work together to create better results. These unofficial collectives led to middle-sized ones and then to large communes.

There were many problems – like lack of infrastructure, electricity and water resource management. The peasants were the manual labor that built any changes that were made. Farmers newly released from years of subjugation produced new social problems as well.

In 1958 the People's Commune was born during the Great Leap Forward movement, when Mao Zedong realized that the country had to industrialize to protect itself. One step was steel production. Mao also mobilized peasants to undertake huge water projects during the slack winter seasons in order to improve agricultural productivity.

The people's commune (Chinese:人民公社; renmin gongshe) was the highest of three administrative levels in rural areas of the People's Republic of China during the period of 1958 to 1985 until these were replaced by townships. Communes, the largest collective units, were divided in turn into production brigades and production teams. The communes had governmental, political, and economic functions.

Eating together in a commune

Each large commune was a combination of smaller farm collectives, consisting of 4,000-5,000 households, and larger ones could consist of up to 20,000 households. These centralized systems, though providing health, education and welfare, also meant that everyone ate together and privacy was extremely limited. The commune system be came deeply resented by its residents.

During the Cultural Revolution, students and educated people were sent to the farms to help the farmers, and to learn from them the simple way of life. Though the students may have enjoyed this time away from study, the educated deeply resented this. The end of the Cultural Revolution saw a surge in the development of agricultural economy, but the farmers remained disadvantaged, with the bulk of the market going more and more to processed foods, not fresh produce.

In the 1990s, after the reforms brought in the market economy, the villages were set back considerably again, because they were unable to market effectively. Dr. Wen feels that the reforms were no longer benefiting rural communities, especially in central and western China, and in some ways hurting them. The success of free market and globalization policies in the short term threatened the long-term viability of China's farm families and villages, by eroding the remnants of the Mao-era communes, which had at least provided health, education, and welfare, leaving individual families vulnerable.

In addition, urban expansion has driven up land prices and local officials confiscated land in order to build factories and housing for the newly affluent. By the middle of the 1990s, there were widespread protests against the corruption of local officials, pollution from the factories (many of which were owned by outside interests), and the gap between the newly rich and the still poor rural areas kept widening.

This gap between the city and the rural poor is what Little Donkey Farm is seeking to narrow. Yan wants to recreate the very old connection between the land and the city dweller as one step on this road.

Yan Xiaohui tells the story of how he found his life's dream at Zhaicheng.

 Yan: I came to Zhaicheng in 2004. I had had a tough time. I experienced searching for my dream and the destruction of that dream. I came to the institute without knowing anything about it. Only that I found a place that could accept me for who I was.

I am from Bauchi, Shaanxi Province. I was the little man in my home from childhood, since my father worked away from home all of the time. I got a very high score of 660 points on my college entrance examination. I could have applied to a very good university but I applied to Northwestern Agriculture University (NAU), which made my teacher, who was very proud of me, very sad.

My reason was very simple. I love nature, so NAU was what I wanted. And it was near my home.

I was not a good student. I spent a lot of time and energy in the environmental protection club and at social events. I made a lot of friends and learned to use the computer very well, but my study lagged behind. So by the winter break of my third year I had to decide whether to catch up or give up.

After the winter I decided to leave the university. Instead, I thought it best to look for a job and a career that would help me realize my life dream: to protect the environment by lessening the impact of society on nature. Giving up my studies was not an impulsive action. I used the whole winter vacation to think about how to continue on my life path. I knew that the university education could not give me what I wanted.

My first job was in a hotel in Xian. I was responsible for the environmental management of the hotel. I wanted to realize my dream. I wanted to be rigorous about this. But when hotel profit was weighed against environmental standards, profit always won. I found that for the hotel, environmental protection was just a slogan and promotional advertising for the hotel. I quit my job.

There was a famous environmental protection expert in the same community. We had cooperated together while I was at university. The man found out that I left school and invited me to work with him. This was sublime, I thought.

But I soon found that his NGO was just for show. In that organization, there was a hidden agenda. So there was nothing of substance. Like finding a beautiful coat but when you open it and the inner lining is moldy and stinks. A person's behavior represents the soul of the organization. I left in despair.

I next found a job in a very popular Internet company. At first I was very happy. I felt good about our team, which was full of young, talented people. But soon that uncomfortable feeling came again. I felt I could not bear the strong commercial atmosphere there.

The first thing we did in the morning was read the company book and recite some relevant parts. Then people would give passionate speeches about working hard to realize their life dream. These speeches always ended with slogans, and these slogans always referred to living in a very expensive community or buying certain brands of cars. These were the symbols of success.

All the people on the stage were inspired by such goals. They were so excited that their faces were bright. I thought, it is okay to make money, but do we need to be so aggressive? Could we be more peaceful and not emphasize material desires so much?

I talked about this with my boss. The boss had much experience and had helped so many people. He agreed with me. Although he also recognized the problem, there was nothing he could do about it. He advised me to stop thinking about it after our talk and to not talk about it with other colleagues. So I quit.

Dropping out of school. Quitting, quitting and quitting. Some said I was totally mad. Others said that I had so much talent and I could have earned several thousand yuan there. People told me, "It was such a good place and we could never get hired there. Why did you leave?" Other people's confusion magnified my loneliness. The dream no longer existed in my mind. And the true reality I wanted to help bring about was gone. No place could fit my requirements and no friend could understand me. I was desperate.

I cried and cried when I called my girlfriend. "Life has no meaning to live like this," I said. "Why can I not find a place that will accept me? What is wrong with the world?" My girlfriend took the train for 8 hours to come to see me. My friends said to calm down and think about where else you can go. Who has similar ideas and where they put them into action. There must be jobs you want.

Then my classmate Huang Zhiyou came home from the institute and said to come back with him. He said he bet I'd like it there. I didn't know what it would be like. I decided to go back with him.

I told my girlfriend, that if I went and didn't like it, I might have to become a beggar. She said she would accept me even as a beggar. We could share what I got from begging.

I went home before going to the institute. My mother trusted me and understood me as usual. And asked nothing. I said to her I was going to Hebei Province and I didn't know when I would return. I left all of my things at home and went to Hebei.

At such a critical time in my life, I appreciated all this friendship and love. People gave me the most important things – understanding and concern for me.

I came to Zhaicheng with nothing. I said when I saw the smiling faces of the people who welcomed me that I felt like I was home.

A young heart is like a tree in growth. When a tree is still young, maybe a gust of wind can destroy it. It is difficult for a lost young man to bear all the choices alone. I felt lucky that I had so many good friends. And such a good girlfriend.

The second day I began to do some farm work. This is what I came here to do. It was autumn and harvest time. I worked and sweated a lot until sunset. A group of us young people then talked until midnight. About spiritual love and physical love.

I was an idiot who knew nothing. But I learned by being here. I knew what was the Yen Yangchu Agricultural Institute. From Dr. Wen Tiejun, I learned what was organic agriculture. From Xie Yingjun, the architect from Taiwan, I learned about eco-building construction. And how to build houses cooperatively. I became his assistant and helped him spread the concept of eco-building.

This should have been the happiest time in my life. But then my girlfriend asked me to leave the institute and come back to her. I couldn't leave, so we broke up. I became silent. I just smoked.

One night I realized something important. I will be here my whole life, I realized. Even if the institute ceases to exist, I will continue to do this.

That one night I composed this poem – my vow to the land and to my companions with deep gratitude:

> I gave up study.
> Summer and winter,
> I harvested confusion.
> Now I farm.
> We talk together in the evening
> Around the stove,
> And I believe in the future. [6]

This is Little Donkey Farm. Not just any old organic farm but a way forward, a lantern in the dark.

Yang Ke, A Platform for Public Dialogue

I met Yang Ke at a conference on Education for Sustainable Consumption (ESC) held at Beijing Normal University in December 2010. The conference is part of an ongoing research program between Japan, South Korea and China. The program is organized by the Institute for Global Environmental Strategies (IGES). She attended on behalf of the Ministry of Environmental Protection where she is an associate research fellow at the Center for Environmental Education and Communications. During the conference Yang Ke spoke about her public education platform interactions with the public, and about programs to help young people learn to fight off bombardment from advertisers.

Yang Ke at a nearby park

This government is listening to the advice of its citizens? This government is trying to help people become smart consumers? It went against what I assumed. Naturally I was curious. I knew that netizens were engaging with the municipality and the central government on a variety of topics. I just hadn't come face to face with someone who was part of it.

Yang Ke represents government efforts we don't always see or may prefer not to acknowledge. It sometimes seems safer to feel part of the suffering masses (so you're not disappointed, again) and to disparage government. Chinese are as quick to complain as Americans about how things are done. We always feel that someone else should do better. This is not to say that government, the Chinese one or any other, isn't sometimes sordid, corrupt and can act against the common good. However there are also hardworking people who are professionals at trying to help.

We met in a coffee shop near my apartment. Yang Ke is smart and dedicated to creating the right kind of future, and that dedication is expressed today by helping me better understand the direction and efforts of her government.

*****

Yang Ke: Our government announced recently that China would move towards becoming an "ecological civilization." There are lots of people doing things already under this umbrella. The government, ministries, education, media, institutions, people – we are all somewhere inside this concept.

We do those things we can do for now – during this time when everything is out of balance. For instance, someone may come up with an idea but it is not really practical or doable now. Like "What Beijing needs are electric cars" and "This is the way our city should go." But electric cars are not sustainable right now. How could we produce enough electricity to run so many cars this way?

We have a lot of conflicting ideas about which way to go. Which way is forward? Or which ideas that are philosophical or value-based ideas are best, like going back to Confucius, Taoism, or the Doctrine of the Mean. "This is the way to get to such an ecological civilization," will be what many will say.

Everyone who is in government is thinking about this now. In the Chinese traditional system, there was one direction given and everyone moved forward together towards it. But now, we need biodiversity; we need different people to explore alternative ways to make a sustainable life. We can think globally but we should act locally. And this is the way it should be.

There are also opinions from outside – from your views – what can make China better. Maybe we do things based on our background and our knowledge. But you see the solution in another way. Different people have different expectations and points of view. Maybe we believe if we follow this way or that way, there will be a certain result. You disagree because you have had an experience with this idea and you got another result. Your experience can contribute a lot. You can be critical and we can adjust our concepts accordingly.

For example, China is now very ecologically focused – we have this concept – ecological civilization – but what do these words mean? At our center we encourage people to think, so we can explore and the words can take on more meaning.

I graduated from Beijing Normal University with a Masters in Environmental Education. I attended classes by Zhang Lansheng, the eminent environmental scholar. He is a great teacher. His wisdom and kindness inspired me. His lectures opened my eyes and I decided to apply for an M.A. I was given the chance to study in Britain and learn what education is like in the rest of the world. When I got back, I was asked to work for the Ministry of Environment.

I always had some connection with nature. In Chinese traditional culture, we are taught that we should work within with our natural environment and that people should be in harmony with nature. That this is how the world really works best.

I see a lot of things in our traditional culture that relate to the Chinese relationship with nature. For example if you look at our traditional paintings, major books or poems, they all describe this importance – that our hearts should be in harmony with our environment. Buddhism, Confucianism and Taoism all teach this. But it is older than these influences.

People feel concerned now … well not everyone is the same anymore as when I was young. Today's young people, their living situation is different. It is more modern. I grew up much more naturally. There was no pollution. I know what natural is.

My grandparents and parents were born before 1949. Life was not so easy. They spent a lot of time looking for food, trying to make their lives more comfortable. It was expected that we make full use of foods we ate. For example, when I grew up and we prepared vegetables, the outside was for the chickens and the inside for us. We didn't have money.

So my life was more integrated with nature than the world is today, especially in the city. At that time there was not so much homework. Maybe we studied 5 1/2 days a week. My sisters, brothers and friends, we'd just go out and play in the village. I was part of the land. I knew the names of the birds and trees, and when flowers bloomed.

Many values and lessons come from our lunar calendar. We have more than 5,000 years of agriculture here. Our Chinese calendar told us what to do when. It was very important, because most of us were farmers, and our parents needed to pass this wisdom down to their children. Otherwise, life would be even harder because their children wouldn't know how to grow things and could starve.

We needed a strong body and learned ways to keep ourselves healthy. Every kind of knowledge was to help us survive or live better with the land. For the farmers themselves and for their children. Our geography, including our climate, made us who we are. But we are industrialized now, so we have lost a lot of this connection and understanding of life.

Our Public Education Platform

Stephanie: Can you explain about your platform?

Yang: The Ministry of Environmental Protection has a national center website and each province and major city has its own website. The national center has the Center for Environmental Education and Communications (SEEC) of the State Environmental Protection Administration (SEPA) of China. It is in both Chinese and English.

Our center was established in May 1996 as the support organization responsible for environmental publicity, education and training. It also functions as the Department of Environmental Technology Exchange and Public Education of the Sino-Japan Friendship Center for Environmental Protection. Its major tasks are to develop activities concerning national environmental protection publicity and education, and train personnel in this regard.

Its major responsibilities are: making and carrying out plans for annual events as well as national environmental publicity activities; organizing the compilation and production of publicity and educational materials, teaching materials and audio-visual products concerning environmental protection, including a relevant database; to make programs and plans for on-the-job training for provincial and local directors and bureaus, and compiling teaching materials and research, certifications, international exchange and cooperation, including a database so Corporate Social Responsibility donors and practitioners can connect.

Beijing has its own website. This localized platform helps people think about environmental problems in the city and use this energy to help make things better. We develop video programming, access television stations, and provide radio programs as well. If you want to know what is happening in big cities in environment protection, what students, businesses or environmental organizations are doing, visit our websites.

We have many, many NGOs that are listed on our websites. We provide ways to connect to funding. We work with them when they have events, and they help us disseminate information and develop awareness about our activities.

Stephanie: What is an example of something from your website?

Yang: Every day you can see new information or programs on our websites. What people are doing today. For example, take June 3, 2011. You can read about:

- 120 Chinese and foreign gardens will be established around the Yongding River;
- This year the city will build five recycled waste projects;
- E-waste recycling campaign held at Tsinghua University;
- Environmental education for primary schools announced;
- Beijing water shortage approaching the limit as the most "thirsty" big city

You will see from these topics that there are many different approaches to public conversations. What we offer is just a platform. It is like different kinds of flowers blooming. At first there is nothing, but if we can provide soil, water and nutrients, seeds will find their way there, grow and become trees or flowers. They are different but it is good to be different.

Stephanie: This is very much in line with the traditional way of thinking. The ancient hope of Datong, or harmony through diversity. How does it connect to Marxism and the PRC?

Yang: This platform between the government and citizens began in 1997. In 1972 the Chinese government attended the Stockholm United Nations Conference on the Human Environment. When the officials returned, they set up a working group for environmental protection. This was a huge and unusual decision for the central government to pay attention to this, since from the Communist point of view, there could be no problem in a socialist society. But they realized that no matter what kind of government you have, you have to face reality. That working group became a committee and in 1976 they set up the ministry.

As a society, we normally seek opinions from experts. Back then we didn't have these new problems. Environmental problems then meant disasters such as floods, earthquakes and famines, and we used our traditional knowledge to work on these. As we became industrialized, human beings influenced the ecosystem more strongly. We added pollutants and such but didn't have the experience to deal with their effects on our wellbeing.

We felt that if we didn't industrialize, our Chinese civilization would cease to exist. You had guns. You had armies. We could only grow food. We could survive by ourselves if left alone. But you are much stronger. We have been invaded many times, and we realized that we needed to industrialize to protect ourselves in this new age. So we learned how to industrialize from you.

Nowadays we need to learn how to solve our environment problems, so again we are learning from you. But some of you now don't have answers either. For this reason, we now want to turn back to our own culture. Listen to our own culture and the experience of our people. We actually don't want to be on your Western train, but we are already on it. How can we get off your train now?

In my job, as a research fellow, my responsibility is to collect information from the West so that people here can see what other people are doing. Today many young people are busy with their own daily lives. They are working to earn money. They are worried about how to make their life better. They don't have time to think about these things. They don't have the time or the heart to think about it. In their life experience everything comes from the big supermarket and they think that is the way life is. As for these big issues – they feel they can do nothing about them. "I can only follow my own road," is what they would say.

What I can do for them is spread this information on the platform to encourage more people to study the problem or think of some way they can make changes in their own lives and influence the people around them too.

Confucius said that only when people have enough food will they take time to be polite. Why did so many people damage the environment, our food security, encourage unhealthy consumption, to become rich? Because they were poor for so long. When they get enough and feel secure, then at that time education becomes desirable. If they get enough education, they will begin to think, "Maybe I don't need so many things."

Right now we are involved in a UNEP project about sustainable consumption – to help young people realize that they are too influenced by advertising. To encourage them to think more about culture and ethical issues.

For example, if you buy a very cheap cotton T-shirt, you should realize that in the south somewhere someone has had to work very hard to make it and for very little pay. We also talk with them about the things businesses do to attract young people even when their products are very harmful to health and the planet. In this project we help them to learn to critique food advertisements. We want them to know what is behind selling these beautiful products.

The Public Conversation

Stephanie: The microblog is huge now. How do you use it?

Yang: We started microblogs two years ago. We used them to develop the idea of a green Olympics to encourage Beijing Municipality to set up a greener environment. We like to use large events since they are a way for people to learn and take action themselves. People did just that.

The foreign media criticized the air quality of Beijing during the run-up to the Olympics. So the government wanted to improve it. The ministry wanted to improve it not only for the Olympics, but also for everyone afterwards. We knew that Beijing had serious problems but didn't know how to capture the attention of Beijingers.

I remember even in 1996 there was a lot of smog in Beijing. We used on this issue and gave financial support to help the city control the smog. We removed the "breadbox cars," those yellow boxy cars with cheap exhausts, in 1997. This was a policy decision. Ten years ago we were so proud to have a big steel factory right in the city. Now we had them move out of the city. Other factories as well.

Events like the Olympics will force people to think about what kind of city they want. Events – they are like a vitamin injection – it encourages the whole system. (*Much of Asia uses injections of vitamins and minerals to help heal colds and minor illnesses.*)

We also hold many activities in schools every year. We prepare leaflets about what schools and students can do to save energy and water as well as how to dispose of waste the right way.

The platform has become our way to interact with the public.

Platform Influences

Yang: Our Beijing platform recently asked an outside organization to do research on its effectiveness. How has awareness about the environment grown in the public? In the report they said that in the last five years that people's awareness has increased. When they asked, "Do you think citizens get enough information about these issues," people responded that they were getting more and more.

There was another international survey. They did a survey with one indicator about citizens' satisfaction with environmental information. Were they satisfied with the available public information? The organization investigated many cities around China in the survey. Beijing was at the top of this indicator.

Sometimes we use such results to prove that if the government uses its resources to publicize information, citizens will become informed. Using the energy of citizens is a good way to improve the situation. The more knowledge citizens have, the more opinions they will have, and the more they can improve government environmental policy.

For example, in order to improve the air quality, some trucks are now not allowed to go downtown. Some didn't like this policy because it wasn't convenient. Before this policy was issued, we publicized, through our platforms, the fact that we were planning to implement such a policy. At the same time, we published quality information through our various media. Later we sent out a questionnaire and asked the public: "Do you support forbidding those trucks to go downtown?" And most people said yes. This helped the government decide to issue this policy.

Microblogs are also important. We have a formal Beijing microblog. If Beijing Municipality has something it wants to do, it first releases the information through our blog, and then monitors the responses. People also share this information with their friends and everyone can see it on the Internet as well. So you can collect a lot of opinions.

We have found that when you educate people so they understand the situation, and invite their opinions, the result can be very helpful for the government. The public's opinion will influence the policy.

Stephanie: Can you give some examples?

Yang: Take garbage, for example, the government may have a plan that some citizens don't agree with. Perhaps because they want to buy a home and don't want a garbage treatment center nearby. Such people try and block it. But then there are other forces, like experts, who can explain that there are safety issues in such a big city at stake here, because we have so much waste. So we ask: You don't want this garbage in your backyard but where shall we put it? We have to think about how to reduce waste and how to treat it properly so residents are happy and the city can function properly and sustainably. Then we monitor the responses.

In June 20, 2011, there was such a discussion on a private microblog. Environmentalists, netizens and district leaders, as well as experts, joined in the discussion. The discussion was around whether the government should build new garbage incineration plants and whether the government does a good job in garbage classification. In summary, although the Beijing Municipality has done a lot, everyone said it is not enough. NGOs should do more to help too. As for our citizens, they said, we should do our best to cooperate with the government. This problem can only be solved with the combined effort of the government, NGOs, experts and residents was the result.

Yang: If we didn't have a platform, people would just criticize. The platform helps people know the whole story so they will not just think of one part, but about how to solve the issue. They don't want the waste near them, but they realize that the problem needs to get solved. We are a city and as a city we need to decide things not only for ourselves but also for the health of everyone.

Development of Waste Management Today

In 2009, about 669 million tons of daily garbage was produced in Beijing. On average, about 18,300 thousand tons was produced every day. If we use 2.5 ton-level trucks to transport this garbage and line them up end to end, the line of trucks will be as long as 47.8 km, filling the whole Third Ring Road in Beijing.[1]

Beijing has more kitchen waste than any other kind. Getting residents to sort garbage is an ongoing struggle. Beijingers are like New Yorkers. They don't like being told what to do. Daily garbage should be divided into 3 parts: "kitchen waste," "recyclable garbage" and "other garbage." Some 40-60% of the garbage is kitchen waste, which can rot and reek. This garbage should be converted into compost. Beijing is just setting up such a system, and it will be difficult to "make" residents do it. The other garbage, such as plastics, papers, metals and so on, should be recycled or buried.

There are four stages in the development of waste management. The first stage is to maintain cleanliness in order to prevent the spread of illness. The second stage is to achieve sanitation and make garbage harmless to the public. The third stage is to improve the rate of recycling and reuse, and decrease the amount of garbage needed to be disposed of using synthetic methods. The final stage is to build a recycling society like Japan.[2]

There was no garbage disposal system here until 1994, and now Beijing is in the transition stage from the second to the third stage after 17 years of development.

Steps Taken by the Municipality

Beijing Municipal Commission of City Administration and Environment is *going to establish 1,200 pilot garbage-classification communities in Xicheng district this year. After August of 2011, millions of sets of new rubbish cans and bags will be distributed to residents in the pilot communities. These updated household sortable rubbish cans have three sizes and come with attached tops. And all the rubbish bags will be changed into degradable ones.*[3]

Furthermore, three kinds of new garbage trucks have been bought in Xicheng, in order to complete the process of gathering and transporting the sorted garbage to the disposal stations or landfills. Beijing government will be responsible for 40% percent of the funds, and Xicheng district will bear 60%.[4]

In addition, the district governments have done a lot to try to develop residents' awareness as well as help them acquire the habit of sorting their garbage. About 15,000 instructors of garbage classification have been trained and are now in communities in many districts of Beijing.[5] *These instructors will teach residents of the harmful effects of unsorted garbage on the city and neighborhoods, how to sort their garbage, and the regulations put forward by the governments. They have the help of DVD videos and brochures. Instructors will supervise and guide residents to sort garbage correctly.*

Sixty-two-year old Wang Fengqin is an instructor of garbage classification in Zaoyingbeili community, Chaoyang district. She is retired. She became an instructor after a 3-month training. Since then, from 7-9 a.m. and 6-8 p.m. every day, she checks and observes how citizens sort the garbage. She has encouraged residents, and they are now taking responsibility and doing this properly. She also attends meetings in Beijing and gives suggestions about garbage sorting issues from her daily experience. She also goes to kindergartens, primary schools or universities to popularize this effort even in her leisure time. Although her children and some residents don't understand, she is proud of herself. "It is great, because being an instructor of garbage classification lets me exercise every day, and I can make some contribution to the community as well," she said. "There are over 800 garbage cans in this area. With these, the condition of garbage classification is now better."[6]

There are also more and more netizens taking action to improve garbage classification and recycling. Huang Xiaoshan is one of them. A lawyer and environmentalist, he came up with the idea of trash-sorting sheds and proposed it to the city. They are piloting this in Changping district. He was also invited to accompany a municipal delegation to Japan to study the successful models in Tokyo.

My Own Experience

Stephanie: I have my own story to contribute. I live in an apartment compound of about seven buildings. Bob and I, when we arrived, wanted to start sorting our garbage but there was no way to do it. There were already sortable bins around the common grounds but they were never used properly. There was also a truck, operated by migrant workers, for certain recyclable items like newspapers and bottles operated by migrant workers.

We have an ayi (housekeeper) who helps us with household work. She is not from Beijing and complained bitterly when we asked her to try and sort for us. No Chinese sorts garbage, she'd say.

I teach a course on global citizenship and sustainable living skills at Beijing Normal University. I saw in the China Daily, in the fall of 2010, several articles about Beijingers' opinions on how to get garbage sorting started. People gave advice and complained a lot because the municipality was considering fines. Of course everyone was opposed to this.

I asked my graduate students to write a report about the article and offer their own opinion on the subject. Most of them agreed with the citizens.

I took up the subject with a group of friends at a dialogue event to support this important effort and see what other people were saying and feeling. My friends talked about what they were already doing but agreed that the government needs to learn how to help citizens better, not just fine them.

Then lo and behold, in the fall of 2011 there appeared big posters about how *to sort on walls around my apartment compound. Meetings were conducted by the management. People were getting serious! Our ayi even told us about the meetings but we were away and missed them.*

Bob and I decided to talk to the management. Sure enough, a young woman gave us two garbage cans. One for kitchen waste and one for other recyclable waste! Now I carefully put my garbage in the right places. My ayi however, still scoffs at the idea. I have asked my Chinese green friends to explain things to her and she is sorting but still doesn't see the point.

Of course, the bags of kitchen waste, the other recycling, and regular garbage all go into the same garbage can outside near the elevator. Still the stuff is in bags and someone sorts them into bigger ones. So I do believe progress is being made.

Impact of Public Information

Yang: Interaction is healthy. It ensures sustainability. Like in Yuanmingyuan Park. The water of the lake is leaking away. Normally plastic is used at the bottom of the lake, because water is very expensive in Beijing, but the plastic has holes now. Environmental experts severely criticized park officials because it is not ecologically sound to line water with plastic. Our

Illustration by Godefroy Durand on December 22, 1860 depicting the looting

media, through coverage of this dispute, forced Yuanmingyuan officials to listen to others and reconsider.

Constructed starting from the early 18th century, Yuanmingyuan (Garden of Perfect Brightness) was a complex of palaces and gardens that served as a pleasant alternative to the Forbidden City as a place of residence and business for the Qing Dynasty emperors. Unfortunately, it was sacked, looted and razed to the ground by Anglo-French forces in 1860, during the Second Opium War, as punishment for the killing of envoys and troops. The opium wars were attempts by the Chinese government to end the sale of opium by the West. The Park had been the most remarkable concentration of Chinese architectural and artistic treasures outside the Forbidden City itself.

Yang: Another example concerns a very expensive residential block. A company wanted to build a heavy electrical line next to this particular block. These residents did research and understood that there are health risks to living near or underneath powerful electrical lines. Wealthy people have more power to protect their health and they demanded that the company change its plans. Although it had already gotten approved, including the environmental evaluation, the media took up the cry and focused everyone's attention on it. Now the company has had to rethink its plans. Through this publicity, even ordinary people have become aware of the hazards of living under such electrical lines.

Such forces coming to bear on a problem help bring balance. Actually, this is a kind of democratic process. When environmental issues come up, people want someone else to agree with their idea. We need to listen to one another, and then when different ideas come up, we can better choose the best for everyone. This is what it means to be *junzi*. Just believing you have the only worthwhile idea can make you blind.

The most dramatic demonstration of the power of Beijing public conversation has been the public outcry and municipal response to the heavy smog that has covered the city from time to time since November, 2001. The ministry publishes air quality index levels for cities using the PM10 standard, which only measures large particles. The U.S. Embassy uses the PM 2.5 air quality index system, which measures finer particles, the kind that actually is much more dangerous. The smog has been so thick some times that the airport has had to cancel flights and car accidents are frequent. Yet, according to the government's measurements, the air quality was "good," but the U.S. Embassy report was that the readings were "crazy bad," meaning beyond 500 micrograms per cubic meter of air.

Public outcry on the web was so intense that the Beijing Municipal Environmental Protection Bureau has now started publishing hourly updates of PM 2.5 measurements.

Stephanie: What other kinds of changes have been the result of such public conversations?

Yang: We recently had a walking map project. For example, we want to encourage healthy walking. This city has become so crowded with so many cars. It influences air quality. Everyone wants to get places fast, for the convenience – but at the same time everyone wants to be healthy and have good air quality. This is a conflict.

How do we solve this problem? We asked people to think how much they could walk every day for their health. Next came the criticisms. People always criticize. "There are so many cars!" Or "It is too dangerous to walk!"

The Beijing Municipal Center can't build more walkways – this is someone else's job. What we can do is raise people's concern about this. We invited people to think or to suggest something.

"You are a citizen," we said. "We want to know about walks that are green and healthy. We invite you to suggest a walk you think is the healthiest. To enter your suggestion, you need to walk it and prove that it is healthy." We collected 50,000 suggestions. People suggested routes. Where they start and where they end. Then we got a map and selected 10 green walking routes, some downtown and others around the other counties of the city.

Here are two that won:

Which is the best walking route for your health? (top two results) (June 3, 2011)

1. Jianguomen, Chang'an Street, Fuxing Road, to the Shijingshan Amusement Park

Reason: Here you have natural scenery, an architectural landscape, political history and culture, all in one. This walk shows contemporary Beijing. The walk is on a broad sidewalk. It is flat, has facilities, public transportation, and is safe and convenient.

2. Yongding Gate, the North and South Long Street, the Drum Tower Avenue, North Star Road to the Olympic Forest Park

Reason: This route goes from south to north, has interesting human interest sites and natural landscapes, plus and good urban planning and wide boulevards: Jingshan, and the National Stadium (Bird's Nest) and on to the forests and lake of the Park.

This created a new dialogue: how we can improve our road system as well as have a place where people can walk for their health? We invited experts to have a dialogue. Delegates came from different parts of the highway department. They said that this activity forced them to rethink their city planning. "If we only build roadways for cars, this will be a disaster. People need pathways to walk and real sidewalks." The landscape department realized they could provide trees, flowers, and greenery to separate pedestrian walkers from the cars. More green – more air. Another kind of vitamin injection to help people rethink what kind of city, what kind of lifestyle they want.

A Sustainable City?

Yang: The future will be better. Will we ever be a sustainable city? As a citizen sometimes I worry about that. The present reality is a nightmare. Maybe someday there will be no water, no electricity, garbage everywhere – a runaway city.

At those times I think I should ask my husband, for the sake of our child, to move to another place. My friends and colleagues – we all realize these problems exist but we still live here. And more and more people realize this too. We need to work together and create a sustainable system. Most people want their lives to be good here. I mean most of us don't want to have to move somewhere else.

We don't have answers at this time. I am busy doing small things, everyday things. So I don't have time to think about this much. I think many people are like me – we have this anxious feeling and don't know how to talk about it. What kind of life will my son live when he grows up?

It is very important to reach the heart of young people. This is not a very traditional way of thinking. In our culture we don't feel it is proper to be so proud of ourselves. But we need people to be proud of themselves! To be able to say, "I did this!" Whenever I meet young people I always say – "You can do this!" Even if I don't have answers. Even if I don't know how to do it.

Stephanie: It is so refreshing to hear this from a bureaucrat!

Yang: People from Western cultures are allowed to be proud of themselves, especially in the U.S. You are encouraged to discover every kind of possibility in yourselves. So I think this kind of bilateral communication is very important for creating sustainability for the future.

Sometimes we need to be humble, but at other times we need to be proud of what we accomplish. Believe in your own strength. But of course you need the right balance. A *junzi* person knows when is the right time to be proud. *(laughs)* Yes, the right balance.

Organic Farming

Yang: When I talk about organics with my grandparents, they just laugh. "That is what we have growing all these years!" They say, "It won't work – you cannot grow enough food for everyone that way." They have their own experiences. That's why sometimes we have go back a little ways but we can't stay back there. We need to go forward.

Stephanie: Organic farming is very time-intensive. We don't all want to become organic farmers. So we need technology to start to work for us rather than human beings working for a technology that doesn't make our lives better.

Yang: Now in Beijing many women who have a good education are renting land and growing vegetables – just for themselves, for their family. Their husbands earn enough to support the family. It is a very different environment today. The relationship between the farmer and the city is beginning to change. We know now that we have to be able to trust the food we buy.

Organic Farmer Zhang Zhimin is an example of one kind of model for organic farming – biodynamic farming. There are different kinds of models. The Little Donkey Farm citizen gardens, are another. People like these show me that consumers are beginning to change. "Okay, I will buy your products at a higher price. In this way, I support your family and you grow the products and my family eats better food." We need to continue to build up this kind of trust.

In the past we focused on *yin* and *yang*, now we talk about eco-agriculture. You have examples like Obama who still involves his country in conflicts (despite the desire of his family to eat healthy and organically). He doesn't use or can't use harmony to resolve conflicts. You Americans use power. You use guns. Use bombs. So now you understand why we decided we needed to industrialize.

Stephanie: For Americans the issue of the environment doesn't connect so simply with security. And at the same time, at least in the case of Libya, the West became incensed at the threat of Colonel Qaddafi going in and ferreting out the rebels, his own citizens, to destroy them. People felt they had to do something.

Yang: We export more so we can become strong, to protect ourselves. You kill someone to protect others. We are indeed different.

Stephanie: We cannot continue to kill because we can and think that we won't see the effects of such actions on the rest of the human family and on the planet itself.

Yang: If we can all get stronger in dialogue people will hear you. Even amongst the Chinese people, we sometimes don't listen to each other very well. It is very important to actually hear each other.

When I went to Sweden, I learned how to use a model to build common understanding and realizations. It is a pyramid for sustainable development. It involves a pyramid with different sides representing different issues – economy, governance, wellbeing, and environment. People put their concerns on each side. From the base line we worked on ways to connect with another participant's perspectives and find a solution we both liked. And through that exercise we discovered how to reach the top and create a common goal for each side.

Local level people will do what they can to improve sustainability where they are. The other levels, middle and top, can also do this. But you won't find the same solution to suit everyone everywhere – people have different problems and different resources, situations and priorities – but there can be some common values.

Stephanie: Two years ago, in 2010, when I arrived in Beijing, I heard that there were quite a few places to buy organic produce but the people running the outfits could never agree how to work together. Then recently on CCTV –9, the English station here, I heard of another a new organic phenomenon – farmers markets – where several organic farmers bring their produce.

Organized by the Institute for Agriculture and Trade Policy (IATP) they are held now every weekend east of Chaoyang Park, Qinghua West Road, and in the Fanhai Business District. Organic farmers are beginning to work together. Beijing is evolving!

We Need to Let People Choose Sustainability for Themselves

Yang: My son is five years old. He is in kindergarten. We need to have children think about the right way to live too. My kid used to leave the water running after washing his hands. One day I brought him to the river – he likes water. I told him that if he leaves the water running, all this beautiful water might someday disappear. Since then he thinks about saving water more.

In his kindergarten the teachers have taught them to make the water stream like a noodle. It is very practical (*demonstrates by rubbing her hands together*). Now he is careful to make the water like a noodle. Water like a noodle has become natural now. They will do this maybe for the rest of their lives. Sometimes it is little things like this.

My husband recently bought two cars. He likes to have choice. People like to be able to choose how to live. If they are able to choose, then they can also choose the right solution as well. This is an important lesson in governing – forbid as little as possible. People hate to be told what to do. Just like kids. When you say no, the child will do it anyway just to make this point: "You can't always say no to me!"

This happens also in society. So when we communicate with people about environmental issues, we can't just tell them what to do or what not to do. We have to give them choices. People will find the way to solve problems wisely. When we raise kids, we find this to be true as well. Kids can find the balance as well.

We are on different sides, like the pyramid game I spoke about before, but you and I have a common goal. We don't have to agree on everything, but we can accept a common goal. We can't decide how other people should live – but we all need to take seriously the value of biodiversity on our planet and the value of harmony. We need to create a garden we can all live in.

Jim Spear, Sustainable Tourism, Building Design and the 21st Century Village

I met Jim Spear at an activity at the Brickyard that I attended with my husband, Bob. We'd been back in Beijing about a year. With no car, deeply absorbed in our own work, and living outside of the areas where expats gather and interact, I hadn't heard of this new development in Mutianyu. Needless to say, we've been back several times.

Jim Spear and his wife Liang

When I was last in the area, around 1995, I visited the "real" Great Wall – in other words, where it had not been reconstructed nor visited much. We had to cross a frozen stream to reach a section of the "wild" wall and then walk up a slope with no path. I remember commenting at the time, about the pros and cons of National Parks, which regulate such places with a view to safety and convenience. On the other hand, I have never had the opportunity to cross a frozen river since, so I am glad to have had the chance. I also remember an enormous pig crossing the road in front of us as we drove up to the nearest village.

Now the area is much more sophisticated, with "organic" orchards here and there, bilingual signs, interesting restaurants, villages and inns. But the best is the Schoolhouse Restaurant and the Brickyard Eco-Retreat – sustainable tourism nestled inside two separate villages. Expats and Chinese, couples and families, come out a lot – to go hiking up to the Great Wall or unwind basking in the beautiful grounds, great food, warm hospitality. To enjoy the balance that art, a storied building and simplicity bring to the idea of place. All part of a commitment to successful and sustainable tourism and to helping people have a fresh perspective on life.

I didn't want to write a book about just Chinese Beijingers. Expats, who have made Beijing their home, are concerned as well, and want to help the city get better. Jim, walks the talk of the expats who are really contributing. He has learned to find his way along a path that many expats fail to see: He is ready to learn but has a great contribution to make as well. He can make that contribution because he knows how to listen. He has good balance.

*****

Jim Spear: I came to China 25 years ago. In the mid-1980s, I was with Unison International, where I did China investment consulting and sales for a variety of industries, including automotive. After that, my wife and I operated a trading company and were co-founders of ASC Fine Wines at that time. Later I joined Chindex, where I worked in general management, distribution management and sales. It is listed on NASDAQ and established the first private hospitals in China.

After 10 years with Chindex, I had a mid-life crisis. I was close to 50. I ran away and moved out to Mutianyu, where we had a country house. I decided to remodel and rebuild it. Friends liked it very much and then friends of friends liked it too and we got into the business of designing and building homes for people. All of these homes were originally peasant homes. We developed a model that included taking out long-term leases on these peasant properties and paying money directly to the villagers.

About the same time, in 2005 the mayor of Mutianyu village asked to have a meeting with me. He said we let you come into the village and in case you hadn't noticed there are no good jobs here. Young people are moving away. People come to see the Great Wall. They look and they may or may not buy a trinket but then they leave. There is nothing left here. Nobody has ever made an investment in our village. You are a rich American – that is some kind of an oxymoron today – don't you think you should give something back?

I have to admit that it was a peasant Party member, the Party secretary of our village, who kicked me in the pants and got me to start thinking about these issues. And so my wife, Liang Tang, and I along with our friends, Julia Upton Wong and Pein Ming, who spent many weekends with us, took out a long-term lease on an abandoned schoolhouse, which we called The Schoolhouse, and this became the center of our business. The main building used to be Mutianyu's primary school until the schools in our rural Bohai Township were consolidated in the early1990s. The campus and nearby structures lay abandoned until early 2006.

The village council approved the lease after a unanimous vote, allowing the village to lease this part of their collective land to outsiders so we could start our business. We didn't have a business plan. We didn't know what we were going to do. But we had a passion for art glass. So we started what was as far as we know is the first and only hot glass shop open to the public in China.

We thought that people might like to stop and look at craftwork and then have a cup of coffee and eat something. So we started the restaurant and that led us into a whole series of small-scale tourism enterprises with our craftwork, galleries, several restaurants and lodgings, and over a period of years we developed ideas about what it means to be part of the community and make a contribution on a sustainable basis.

The Schoolhouse Properties

Jim: The Schoolhouse Campus has a variety of dining and meeting rooms and a multi-purpose gallery and studio we call the Art Room, where up to

Logo

Brickyard Eco-Retreat

160 people can dine. A number of my house clients have asked us to manage their custom-designed homes, and we offer them for short-term rent to visitors under a program we call "The Schoolhouse Homes." The restaurant and nearby rental homes, offer a unique combination of facilities. You can stay at the homes and then go the Schoolhouse to eat, or get away from it all and spend your time in these luxurious getaways with private gardens & spectacular Great Wall views.

We also own and operate the Brickyard Eco-Retreat at Mutianyu Great Wall, which opened fully in March 2011. It was developed from an old glazed tile factory and we designed it to be green from the ground up. All of our 16 rooms have story-and-a-half window walls and terraces facing the Great Wall. The lushly landscaped grounds also contain a lodge with a fireplace and café, public rooms in what used to be the old kiln as well as a fully equipped conference center, a spa and the garden where we grow the vegetables we serve.

In addition to the Schoolhouse, we also operate Xiaolumian, a tiny noodle shop. This restaurant was created from an old stone farmhouse, and offers handmade noodles and sauces in a private garden with Great Wall Views.

We are committed to sustainable tourism. We qualify as a 4 Green Star from Eco Hotels of the World and were selected as the HICAP best sustainable communities development in Asia-Pacific for 2009. We recently were selected as one of the top 5 hotels in China in 2009 by Wild China. Sustainability is a lot more than a buzzword here.

Our whole family and our friends are involved in The Schoolhouse. We all wear multiple hats. My wife, Liang Tang, is mainly responsible for group/corporate sales and government relations. My daughter Lauren is responsible for housekeeping and reservations. My daughter Emily is a staff artist and guest relations specialist. My mom, Joan Spear, is mostly here now and when she is, she works as a hostess. She is also the owner of Grandma's Place, one of our rental homes. Our partner, Julie-Upton Wang, heads educational and no-profit sales and programs. She also runs the Schoolhouse Art Glass Shop with technical assistance from her husband, Pein Ming.

The Schoolhouse Concept of Sustainable Architectural Design

Jim: How do you take the thousands of years of a tradition in building and design and marry it with modern materials, a more modern aesthetic, a sense of light and a sense of perspective? How do you combine the traditional and the modern? This is what the designs that I do are all about.

This work didn't start from analyzing things first. It came from learning from the local buildings and then figuring out how to open them up. Like the Brickyard. It is a riff on that theme. Keeping something that was old and redeploying it. Keeping the existing Chinese style buildings but opening them up.

That building was featured in *Architecture Technology*, the top Chinese architecture journal. We have had just dozens of architects from literally all over the world come to look at that little brickyard. I never dreamt it. What is most flattering to me – I don't claim to be an architect – I am a designer. What is most flattering to me is that now the local people in the villages, when they have money, when they are rebuilding, when they are redoing their houses, they are taking some of our ideas to make their homes more livable. A luxury of simplicity – you don't need to have a huge house.

Our Concept

Jim: There are two basic principles that we look at in our sustainable tourism concept.

First: We try to use existing footprints.

Buildings that are already there. Instead of tearing them down, we redeploy them to different uses. Whatever we tear down, we save the materials and build something new.

From an ecological perspective this makes a great deal of sense because no matter how energy-efficient new construction is, using the best technology – if you tear something down and throw it away and start over from scratch, it takes 30-50 years to get an energy gain. In today's rapidly changing world climate, 50 years is an eternity.

You have to look at the whole picture. *(elaborating)* The whole footprint. If you have an existing building, it takes energy to tear it down. It takes energy to dispose of the materials. It takes energy to prepare for the new. It takes energy to do the new design, to bring new materials to the site. So when you look at the whole thing – that is a lot of energy. Even though the building is more efficient, it takes a long time with current technology to actually save energy. So until you get 30-50 years, out you've expended more energy. You would have been better off just to keep the original building.

So we keep the original building and use the vernacular architecture. Some of the good things – the slab floors and the overhanging eaves – we retrofit them. We put in energy-efficient lighting, insulation – we do a whole range of things. We don't do everything because, for example, we work from limited budgets with limited amounts of time. We believe that perfection is the enemy of the good enough.

You might wonder why more buildings aren't saved elsewhere. It costs more in terms of upfront investment to keep what is there already because you might need to fix the foundations.

For example, we know some people who have gotten the rights to 25 sq. km of land and want to take six natural villages, tear them down, move the villagers into new villages, and then build lodges on the remains of the old villages. To me this leads to the second principle we have for sustainability.

Second: The built environment exists in a social context.

Jim: The village has families who have been there for 500 years. Families and clans have ties to and affections for the land, and they think of themselves as stewards.

Look at the whole structure of incentives today. For the most part, the deck is stacked against people who want to preserve buildings. Not just in China but in the whole world. We disagree. Our idea is to integrate into existing communities instead of dispossessing and displacing people.

Typically in large projects, the people at the bottom get the rawest deals. They suffer when their houses and land are taken away. Because like other countries, China has the right of eminent domain. This happens all over the world in rapidly developing societies.

We rent using houses that people are no longer using – they have moved away or are unused for other reasons. We have done close to 40 leases in villages around us. And not in a single instance have we displaced a resident.

Ups and Downs of Being in a Chinese Village

Jim: Somebody last year wrote nasty stuff about us in a blog. "The School-house is just a bunch of rich people kicking the villagers out," they said. That was so unfair! I had to reply to it. One concern could be encouraging gentrification. But we have used only 40 of the 400 houses. Besides, we are not taking away houses people want to use or can't afford to live in.

Many people come back to stay with us over and over again. People from overseas too. 40% of those who stay overnight, are Chinese ID cardholders. The villagers live right next to them during their stay with us. Our guests are not used to that!

We have an old man and old lady near our own home, for example. They just scream at each other every day. They both have accents so I can't really understand them. I thought they were fighting. It turns out that they are both going deaf – so they have to yell to hear each other! *(laughs)*

In traditional societies, everyone was a part of a community. As shepherds or farmers, some had a lot more money, some lived closer to the edge. By and large people lived together. Here in China and in the U.S. now, urbanization is organized according to wealth. Today the rich live here and the firemen and police live there. The Hispanic maid lives somewhere else. With this kind of distribution you lose the sense of being people together.

It does take a village. People give us their first cucumbers and such just to be neighborly. They don't want anything. I think that really gets lost when you are in an apartment building in a suburb. You don't really know anyone around you. In a little village you may not know everyone, maybe not by name, but you do by face.

Like this Friday. We've been invited to a wedding. I love the weddings and the 30-day celebrations after the birth of a child. The groom's father, Li Fenghai, was profiled in a book we had written, (Off) *The Great Wall*. His son is getting married and we are invited to the wedding.

For the first part of the wedding, he has hired a traditional wedding troupe with sedan chair and all the noise. Our village is 3.5 km long, and he is paying them to make the circle three times carrying his daughter-in-law. (*He smiles at me delightedly at the thought of the sedan chair and bearers and the noisy drums and horns going up and down the hills and paths of the village.*)

In our village not everyone is nice. We have bad elements. We have family abuse, neighbors help, neighbors call the police. There are disputes among neighbors. You know this kind of thing.

I had to go to Mayor's Court once. This was when we first got to Mutianyu. I thought it was a joke how much people care for their trees. We'd finished our house and we were already living there full time. There came a banging on the door and there was this little old man. And he says you know the pear tree outside of your gate is mine. And your car is pressing down on the roots of my pear tree. I thought that was such a joke.

It was partly true. Because if you take away the air from the roots, the roots will drown and it impacts how much fruit is produced. So there was truth there. Turns out we could settle the issue if we'd pay him a 100 yuan a year. Now our car can park above the roots of his tree.

A couple of years later, I was doing some work on the house and I was getting close to another tree that belonged to the same family. At the end of every day they would come and tear down what we had built. No due process, no court, no legal benefits.

So we asked the mayor to help and he held a mayor's inquiry session. Our family went and the other family went. In the traditional family tradition, the head of household is the man. My wife is Chinese but she is very, very liberated, and so to have to go there and be told by the mayor to be quiet – *(laughs)* – it was really something.

But the upshot was I told my story, and the other guy, Mr. Fu, told his story and the mayor decided we had to compensate Mr. Fu. You know, to get elected, mayors have to listen to the court of public opinion. But they have to make sure they do the right thing. If you have outsiders coming into the village and there are different interests and different understandings… the answers cease to be easy ones.

I had to learn and to respect, to consult and talk with the neighbors about such things. I realized that what I did really had an impact. We actually never got to a court case. We learned how to deal with such situations in every project whether it was a commercial project or a residential house for clients.

We ended up taking a lease on the family's whole orchard that surrounded our house at the top of the hill. About an acre of their land. We also pay them to maintain our orchard, which is mostly chestnuts. Those are the chestnuts that we serve at The Schoolhouse. So we have the family making money, and at the same time, providing the care the trees need.

It is win-win. But I had to be taught. I think it's to my credit that I was willing to be taught. I didn't come into the village and strong-arm them into doing what I wanted. As a matter of fact – to act like a foreigner – that's a recipe for disaster. "I am a foreigner and now I am going to lord it over people." If it was ever appropriate it is no longer, because China is back.

So this social role is part of the built space we have. It is critical to success. If you don't understand this relationship, you get into trouble.

I am like a bull in the china shop, but I learn and I am persistent. So we use existing footprints and stay a part of the community.

The most important way that we identified with the community has been to provide jobs and livelihoods. If you have a job close to home, you don't need to move away. You can stay in your own home.

The Schoolhouse "Rules"

Jim: We have more than 50 full-time employees as well as 20-30 part-time workers. The part-time workers are all farm housewives, as are most of the employees. They have rarely ever had a job outside their home. So their work with us enables them to get their feet wet and get a take-home salary. If you are close to being a subsistence farmer, which is what a lot of these farmers are, then you don't have much cash. In today's society, you got real problems.

Think of it. It is a woman who is bringing home cash to her family – very revolutionary. These are our kitchen staff – except for our wonderful executive chef, Randhir Singh. We give them good jobs. We have very little turnover.

We pay employees 12 months a year, we follow the rules, and we provide benefits – that is a social responsibility too. It is not a sustainable business model to cheat your employees. It is not a sustainable business model to try to evade the letter of the law or even the spirit of the law. I may not like it but I don't have the right to say, well, the law should be this or that, and operate outside the law. If you have a business model that doesn't let you to pay your people according to the law – this is not sustainable.

We have direct employees and 100-odd people, at any given time, including the permanent staff of our Cleaning and Gardening Service. I have to come up with cash to pay salaries and benefits every month. That's a big responsibility. And then there are local businesses and contractors that we prefer to hire. Our township has only 10,000 people, and we are the biggest employer.

Stephanie: What is it like running a sustainable business in China?

Jim: We have a whole class of employees who are permitted under Chinese labor laws to work part time. There are a lot of protection laws in place in China. We are not required to pay benefits but there are strict limits about the number of hours they can work and the compensation that they can have. This is fair. You know the Chinese know that in our country there are many big companies who use part time employees so they don't have to pay benefits. So, they want to protect their workers.

The rules here are probably overbalanced in favor of the employee because of an ideological bias and you can understand where that comes from. Whereas if you look at my country, the law is overwhelmingly in favor of the employer. And so where is the balance point? You have to have rules. And then you work at making the rules operate better. I think people in the U.S. tend to have a telescopic view of our very short history. If you go back to 200 years – who could vote in the U.S.? You better be free, white, and a 21-year-old male property owner.

I don't mean to be crude about it but it just takes time to develop a sound system of labor laws. I know from my own experience in China, and I studied Chinese political economy at Berkeley and quite a bit of Chinese history. What I learned in academia certainly has informed and helped me as I lived here and done business. Things are pretty good here and they are getting better. It doesn't mean that things that are bad are okay. But you don't throw away the baby with the bathwater.

It seems to me that both societies have some work to do on this. It is not so much what the rules are but more how they are operationalized. What is the actual practice?

We know that in certain places in China there are abuses of employees. Employers who are not playing by the rules. There are lots of breaches of laws and corruption in certain places. But that is why there is the law, why there is public opinion, why there is concern and outrage when there are abuses.

It takes time to make things better. So, in a little company like ours, the burden is high. The concept of having a living wage with some security in their lives, and which comes from the private sector – I think that this is a sound structure that can develop. It is tough for me to live up to that structure but it is the right way to operate.

Stephanie: The value of what you do, your sustainable practices, this influences your community as well. Employing people who never believed they could earn cash. And the software – the relationships you've built with the villagers. The fresh ideas come from your creative thinking, as well as from your guests. I'll bet they've learned to respect you too.

Jim: I think people know when you are sincere and working hard and not trying to run a scam. I also think that there is a tremendous reservoir of goodwill and concern for other people. Sometimes China has gotten a bad rap from incorrect and inaccurate assessments of Chinese culture. Saying that Chinese don't care about other people other than their own family. My experience after going on three decades is exactly the opposite.

I think that as soon as they have enough to eat themselves, they start caring about other people. I think that is human nature. Then there is that wealth of wanting to do the right thing. Does that mean that there is no selfishness? Does that mean that there is no corruption? Of course not.

People think the way to change China is through education. That is a truism, but I cannot abide it when I hear that. We have a lot of people who come up and they say, we want to help, we want to go to the school here and they think that that's the big social issue. Well, in our area they have beautiful schools. They have good teachers. They have good education. Families take what resources they have and they put it into education so their son doesn't have to be a farmer. They have been doing that since history in China began.

Going to the schools is so fake – so white man's burden – you can quote me on that – it's looking down and saying I am the big rich foreigner. I am going to come and play with you for a few minutes and take some pictures and make myself feel good about it. We don't want anything to do with that.

As a business, when you do things for charity, you do it publicly because the benefit that you get from it is public. And if you do things as an individual, maybe the best kind of charity is what is kept quiet.

But as a business we can select what we support. We support our programs for poor people and the elderly – because that is the social issue in our area. The social network falls apart when the kids grow up and move away. And the old people are left there and they are infirm. They can't get to the doctor. They can't take care of themselves. They have no cash incomes and sometimes there are family disagreements and the old people are abused. It is not just China – it happens all over the world.

Stephanie: What to you is doing sustainable tourism the right way?

Jim: We look at tourism as a means to a sustainable livelihood. I spoke before of the people who bought 25 acres of land and will destroy what is there and build anew. We researched about sustainable tourism and discovered that large-scale tourism is extraordinarily destructive for communities and very few benefits stick. The people who get the least out of such tourism are the poor.

It turns out if you have small-scale development, more stays with the local community. There are more jobs; there are more opportunities for small-scale entrepreneurship and so on. From the very beginning we wanted small scale as a business. This means high cost because you can't spread it around very far.

That is why we elected to have multiple small front ends that fit into the local communities. The Brickyard, for example. That front end is at the scale of the local community and hires people from the local community and uses existing buildings. We didn't kick anybody out. We didn't raze the village.

What we have as a business model is we have common management, we have accounting systems, and we have procurement systems. We can then spread the overhead across the front ends. This makes it feasible as a business. Again, if you are in a business, and you can't make a go of it economically, it is unsustainable.

I am believer in enterprise. I am a believer in unleashing the creativity of people. There needs to be some self-interest that gets engaged. But there are other kinds of self-interest other than making money. Still from a business perspective, you need to make a profit. "Do I have enough cash to pay my bills?" is an important reality that doesn't go away.

A lot of times, government programs and non-profits are aimed at a particular project to relieve poverty or create development. All of which is tied to a grant. But when the grant money dries up, the whole thing blows away. That is a major problem. You have now moved two steps forward and three steps back. All the people who you got excited about it are left with nothing when the grant runs out. What was all that passion about – all that love?

You need to think carefully about programs that help small businesses. Micro-finance has turned out to be a scam for many. It is not very pretty. Not to say there wasn't a very good germ. It was there to begin with but for the most part, it has been implemented by people paying themselves well to rip off poor people.

I don't rip off poor people. I pay living wages to poor people. I am a little self-righteous about this. I am proud to run a business that people can be proud of working for.

Of course, a sustainable business has to work, just like a regular business. People need to want to buy what you are selling. It is not enough to build a better mousetrap. You have to let people know you have a better mousetrap. We also have a lot of issues in our local area because we have resource limitations. We have management limitations, for example.

But I learned. My management skills changed, both my Western ones and the ones I honed here. Live long, learn long, the Chinese say. Maybe I am a slow learner, but I keep getting surprised. Hardware is easy in the sense that if you have money and a good designer, you can create something. The real issue is software – people – and people are complicated. I spent my whole career in business, so I know you need to put people first.

People may not like the way you put people first. Because it flies in the face of their expectations and their previous experience. For example, there are many local businesses that don't provide the benefits that are mandated by law. And we do.

Employees too will come and want to cut a deal with us. You pay me more and we will skip the benefits and you can save money and I can make more money. When I say I am not going to do that, people think I am stupid.

Or I have people all the time saying they want us to provide them with net salaries. We don't do that. We provide all of our salary compensation on the basis of gross salaries. People are responsible for their own share of taxes and benefits. If you pay net salaries, people lose the connection that the government is making them pay a contribution to their own benefits. We are very clear about this. We are very insistent about this. And then people think I am stupid. I may be but I am also stubborn.

It is not a sustainable business if you talk out of two sides of your face. I can't do that. To learn and change course if need be, but I refuse to be bothered by such things like cutting side deals on the benefits.

You have to have some amount of basic principles. At the Schoolhouse, since it was a school, we have what we call our ABCs: Respect people, obey the law and provide our guests with pleasant experiences. If you are really doing that and really operationalize it, then it really means something. It is not just a slogan. We also have a number of sustainability principles that go from design to operating principles that connect beauty with sustainability – because beauty matters.

I respect people around me here. There is a deep appreciation for beauty and a connection between beauty and the earth here. Growing things is a kind of beauty. People here don't just grow vegetables. They grow ornamentals, they grow flowers. They care for vining rose bushes, honeysuckles and forsythia and not just what was planted by the government. Although the government has done a lot and it is just gorgeous. Sometimes the sense of beauty is different. There is the old saw that beauty is in the eye of the beholder.

The 21st Century Village

Stephanie: How do you support the village of Beigou, where the Brickyard is?

Jim: The Brickyard is the first business Beigou has ever had – they never even had a farmer's household home-stay program like other villages in the area. The current mayor was born there and came back after a career in the army, where he had the opportunity for education and travel. Isn't it cool that the person with the most smarts and the most education and the most gumption can get to be the one who becomes the leader? I respect him tremendously.

First he took a courtyard house and started a village cooperative and home-stay program. It is clean and it is nice. Then there was an abandoned village hall. He turned it into a restaurant called Beigala. He got recipes from the village housewives and now they take turns staffing it. He's hired a full time chef and attracted a full-time manager to come to the village and run it.

We send people to eat at his restaurant all the time. People like to eat at our restaurants too, but people want choice. They want the opportunity to experience the authentic thing. So we send them there. We helped with their English menu. It is just up the road from the Brickyard.

We suggested to him that there ought to be rental bicycles, but that we weren't looking to start such a thing. So his cooperative started a bicycle rental program.

The government has also helped a lot. They allocated funding for hiking trails and roadways so people can get around easier. They've landscaped and put in sewers. We've had so many meetings with the township people about such things.

I've asked government people their opinion about what it means to build a better life for these people. What is a better life? It can't just be about becoming a gas-guzzler and an energy waster and stuff like that. How can you expect the villagers to stay? They want better livelihoods and wellbeing.

If you want people to stay in their villages, you gotta must deliver the 21st century to them. And the 21st century doesn't mean tearing down everything that is there. It doesn't mean tearing down villages and putting up a parking lot. People hate being disrupted from their lives. And there is a groundswell of dislike for the kinds of programs that kick people out.

People in the government are really and truly interested in what is happening up here. I see that in the support and the attention we are getting from them. It is not that we have answers for everyone. China is a huge country with perhaps 650,000 villages, so there must be a lot of different approaches.

That is one of the wonderful things. Over the last 30 odd years since the opening up *(when Deng Xiaoping became the "chief designer" and China opened up to the world)* there has been a tremendous willingness to experiment. To try something new and to see what works and what doesn't.

That spirit is really important and it could be used a lot more than just in China. This issue of urbanization and depopulation of poor rural areas is all over the world. They can't get enough tax revenue to support those who still live in villages nor deliver social services on a sustainable basis. It ain't just China. Look at my own country, the States, and go to rural mountainous areas and it is the same.

Recently, Beigou's Mayor Chen had a village meeting to celebrate the village's new status. He invited me as well as the new foreigners who hadn't gotten their honorary certificates yet. I've had mine for quite a while, of course.

Beigou has just been selected as the most beautiful village in Beijing, and CCTV did a documentary on the village. The mayor was also selected as one of 10 model village Party secretaries in the country. He is a sharp and savvy guy.

He showed the CCTV documentary and, of course, the Brickyard was in it. He thanked me and said at first people didn't understand what I was trying to do. Now they know that I have the interest of the village at heart.

Beijing and the Right Urban Design

Stephanie: And Beijing proper?

Jim: Last year I was asked to speak at a government round table that had people from the Cultural Relics Bureau, and famous old professors and architects. I was the lone foreigner who was asked to go – because I am building things here.

The topic was how do we make Beijing into a world-class city that still has local characteristics. I think that is a big issue all over the world. It is a funny thing. If you go to places that are very poor, there is a similarity to poverty that is discouraging. At the same time there is a similarity to modernity that is depressing. There is an ugliness to homogenizing everything. There are not many cities in the world that have found the right balance. To work like a modern city and still have a past. Paris is one of the better ones.

At this round table I said not to forget the beauty of authentic architecture and look for authenticity for your future. In Beijing think of Pingandadao, where they cleared out a whole strip to create another Changan Avenue (*the main street that divides the city between north and south*). Where they have built fake Chinese buildings on both sides. Terrible. There is no soul. There is nothing that speaks to their innate sense of beauty. It is fake, just fake.

You can appreciate the shape of the CCTV tower but I don't think there is anything Chinese about it. And is it fair to say that there should be something Chinese? Maybe not for everything, but there should be room for real Chinese architecture.

Form has to fit function. Chinese are just as capable at doing this. That is why this is such an exciting time. I have cooperated with a Beijing heritage and cultural protection foundation. They create salons and focus on preservation architecture. A few years ago they brought out a number of architects to look at what we'd done. One of the architects was a young Chinese architect from Guangdong who trained in the U.S. at Berkeley. He was for six years an assistant to I. M. Pei. He now has his own firm in Beijing.

I am an enabler, and a positive one, I hope. I get to provide opportunities for other people. To put their creativity and energy into something and give it voice. I have managers or work with other builders or architects. What a wonderful thing when someone creates something. We have interns who write books. We do fellowships. We do a lot of stuff. We give them 30 days of residency. This is just the right thing to do.

Not a Fanatic but Moving Towards Biodynamic Farming

Jim: To get the big picture you have to get the small picture and start putting the pieces together. And you have to experiment and play at it persistently.

Take food. We operate three restaurants. Our theme is local, homemade from scratch, but we don't have a fetish about it. People like wine from around the world. People like coffee and we get our coffee from Yunnan. It is not fair-traded but we are sure that the people who farm it get a decent living. The company was established with UNDP support. It passed the blind test so not only is it sound from a goods perspective, it also tastes the best. And that is why we picked it. We had an intern from Belgium, and he spent the whole time looking at the Fair Trade issue in China and teaching us about it and to be quite honest, they are not there yet.

We grow our own vegetables and we grow them on land that had been abused for a long time – so can we say our food is organic? We can say that we grow food according to organic principles. But the land was ruined and it takes a long time to clean it up.

But we're not interested in testing it and getting a certain certification as organic. There is a legal definition that operationally may be a scam. It is industrial organic.

We want to be as much organic as is reasonable and practical – without having to get into denial – like it is so much better to be poor – gimme a break – why can't we have a few luxuries? Throughout human history there has been a trade in luxuries. I run a restaurant. If I don't have Coke, people won't come. Or if I don't have coffee, they don't come.

We compost and we put back into the land. And over time the quality of the land gets better. We procure from other local suppliers who are known to grow on a small scale, we even go to the extent of ordering things from individual peasant families. We have people who forage for us and then we pay them.

We have a bigger project that will take us to the next step. An entirely bio-dynamic farm. Biodynamic is what you are really talking about here when you are looking for truly organic. Not just local, or organic greenhouses. Biodynamic means that you don't have external inputs but that you take food to feed people out of the land.

So, actually, a biodynamic farm creates a surplus and that is what is really cool. You don't have outside inputs – you don't put fertilizer in – it is not just the soil, it is an integrated production cycle.

We did an investigation. We went to a place in northern California called the Philo Apple Farm.

They are wonderful people – they have a 30-acre apple farm that is run according to biodynamic principles. The family who started it that actually started the famous French Laundry Restaurant, now owned by Thomas Keller. They got farther out of the wine country and into the boonies and found a century-old apple orchard. And then they revitalized it.

They do cooking classes and have four little cottages. They grow their own food and have animals – goats to make cheese and milk, and horses. They take the manure and put it back into the land. Everything is integrated. There are a lot of experiments like this.

This is what our staff ecologist did her master's thesis on. She spent two years working on a demonstration biodynamic farm. We'd like to go towards fish, hog and corn production. We are not all going to become vegetarians but we should all eat less meat.

Biodynamic farming is a method of organic farming that focuses on symbiosis. The farm is a whole system of interrelationships – soil, plants, animals. The system becomes self-nourishing. In other organic agriculture, some assistance for the farm comes from outside, for example, organic fertilizer, composts and seeds. On a biodynamic farm all of this is produced within the farm.

So we are moving in this direction, but this will take time and the purchase of more land.

Stephanie: What can China demonstrate to others about sustainable city ideas?

Jim: I think we need to realize that we can get more out of less if we are intelligent. Use less and get more. And there may not be a natural limit. How much we can get out of the wonderful bounty of the earth and the energy that comes from the sun? There may not be a practical limit for humanity. We ought to be able to deliver the good life. But does the good life mean that we all have a huge mansion?

This doesn't mean you have to be a zealot.

Where does a business fit into a sustainable society? We should be able to do the things we love. I love to be able to travel, read books and stuff. We all make choices. We can make choices that are also good for the planet. Greed is the big killer because it becomes a driving force.

I don't own a car. This is a choice I made but I am not making other people do the same. I call it the luxury of simplicity. If you go to our Brickyard, the rooms are small – there are grass slippers – I mean there are a whole range of things that go together and, in a simple way, create luxury.

I think Chairman Mao Zedong has been much maligned. He said the urban/rural divide is the most important social contradiction and sociologists now have recognized the same thing. In China you have rural residents. They aren't peasants anymore. They've been mobilized and they now need to be integrated into the bigger society. People in the cities, on the other hand, are disconnected from the rhythms of the land. That's why we think we can be selfish about consumption and only think about me, me, me and get away with it.

The worldwide cities are drowning in their own droppings. There are lots of people who have created technological approaches – vertical gardens, rooftop gardens. There are all kinds of things that so far are "also rans." They are not having a big impact yet. But there is hope. There is a lot of hope.

Where is the structure of incentives? What is the government doing to channel the energy in the right way so that the right social energy emerges? Human energy, directed in such a way, and the capital to go with it? So that after 10 or 15 years, life is very different in terms of society and the built environment than before?

There are a lot of things that China may very well be doing intelligently. Look at solar power. You can talk about China taking technology that is developed elsewhere and subsidizing it. For heaven's sake. I hope they are subsidizing solar energy. I think the whole world should subsidize solar energy. I have a client here who has a very large factory for a European company. His whole roof is covered with solar energy panels and they feed into the power grid.

The most important thing here is to get scale. In the U.S. they give tax incentives to rich people to put in solar panels or give tax incentives to rich people to take on small-scale hydro. Spend a dollar to make 50 cents worth of electricity. We don't have the right structure of incentives. You need scale so that the right things become affordable at lower and lower levels. To make it feasible, do the right thing. I think there are some really smart people here who are thinking through these issues.

Do I think any government or institutions can sit, know all and guide perfectly? Of course not, but I think there are things to learn here. And then look at what could be done better elsewhere.

Chinese love cars. They love the open road. They are just like the people in the U.S.. Being a peak industry, China has created the whole economic system that enables cars to be made profitably. Now we are drowning in auto pollution here too. We should increase the price of gas – make people pay to go in congested areas – like in London and Singapore. Discourage the driving.

In China it is probably more feasible because it has made a much bigger investment in mass transit. In the U.S. the people who suffer the most are poor people who have to drive broken-down cars to get to work and they don't have other transit options. But here, there are buses. There are subways. There are more subways and more railroad tracks, and now more freeways, than the U.S. has.

When you take on big projects like these, it doesn't mean that you are not going to make mistakes. It also doesn't mean that there isn't intelligence, or good will, or there isn't commitment. I think China and its leaders here are every bit as aware as people in the rest of the world about the issues we face on this planet and in our communities. They have a huge responsibility, and they know it.

View of the Great Wall from the Brickyard

Professor He Huili, the Rice Professor from China Agriculture University

I met He Huili through Mac. They are both involved in the Community Supported Agriculture (CSA) association here in China. She is a professor of sociology at China Agriculture University, where she trains students to work on the urban/rural divide in China. She is from Henan Province and has several projects in villages trying to help farmers and villages get out of poverty. She is a local official in Lankao, the capital of Lankao County, and was recently appointed a vice mayor of Kaifeng.

The urban/rural divide is of grave concern to many in China. The villages, mostly poor, feed urban residents who are so much better off. This has led to massive urbanization of cities by migrant workers who work the worst jobs, for very little money. But that money is cash and will provide education and conveniences for the families back home. This strain on cities is both social and environmental because resources are strained.

The schools in these villages are full of children whose parents are away creating this cash flow. These students are being raised by their grandparents, but the lack

The Rice Professor

[Professor He Huili, the Rice Professor from China Agriculture University]

of real parenting is causing problems. Recently, the Ministry of Education has been sending teachers into the schools to try and help educate these children. They have upgraded schools as well.

He Huili has helped her villages receive training in organic agriculture, marketing, and cooperative training. She has set up several cooperatives. Progress has been slow. The long-embedded concept, "the cheaper the better," despite the food scandals, is slow to die. The idea that people should pay the true price for good produce is one that is very far away from the normal reality at the market. Distrust and disdain on both sides of the farmer-consumer relationship is a major problem even in the nearby cities of Lankao and Kaifeng, the ancient capital, which is larger and much more cosmopolitan. So it is an uphill struggle.

The farmer and agribusiness focus on getting you the cheapest price – with little concern for food safety. And, although the government recognizes the problem, it also needs to feed 1.3 billion people. People's health is at risk.

Just as in the rest of the world, there is no real consumer confidence in what is being called organic. There is no good system or institution that enables sustainable produce to reach Beijing markets from other parts of the country.

Western-type "farmers markets" are just starting in Beijing. The traditional markets (which were naturally organic for centuries) are conveniently near apartment compounds but they are now supplied with industrially grown produce. Still, food scandals have led to a growing consciousness about the need for healthy produce.

He Huili is a rural sociologist. She has dedicated herself to helping the farmers and the villages in her hometown with the support of her students at China Agriculture University. She wants the villages in her care to develop economically through the adoption of sustainable agriculture.

*****

He Huili: I graduated from Beijing University in 2007 with a doctorate in sociology, specifically urban and rural sociology. It took me six years. I learned about the importance of organic agriculture and creating cooperatives to support it, from Dr. Wen Tiejun, when he participated in a seminar in 2001. I was very moved by his lecture and ever since helping farmers grow organic and healthy food has been my passion in life.

In 2003 I started conducting experiments all over Lankao County, which is my home county. One of these experiments was developing better quality rice, using organic methods, in the village of Nanmazhuang. It turned out that this Nanmazhuang rice was very, very good. We decided to sell it in Beijing.

I worked from Beijing and Mr. Zhang Yanbin, the mayor, from Nanmazhuang. It became the famous rice story. I was called the rice professor here in Beijing. We found a small bookstore named Utopia and brought up the rice to Beijing, sold it and arranged for prepaid orders. We gave speeches at the opening, and many students and teachers came. A lot of journalists came, from television and several newspapers. There were lots of people and a lot of rice.

In my speech I talked about the importance of rural cooperatives and the value of "no public harm" rice. We called it Yellow River Rice since it grew using the water of the Yellow River, which is our motherland river. This story made a very beautiful impression on Beijing residents. Beijing News, Xinhua News Agency and other media ran stories about this "no public harm" rice but the coverage in Henan was small. Food safety was not considered very serious at that time. The idea of cooperatives was an interesting idea to Beijingers but not to the people of Henan. Sales tapered off after the initial rush.

Utopia was too far away for consumers. After a while, the media stopped reporting about us and turned to other hot topics. Sales dropped. The reason I chose the bookstore to sell the rice was so I could give lectures about these new ideas. The audience consisted mostly of the intelligentsia, people who wanted to talk about the issue, not buy the rice. In the end only about 100 people went to the bookstore and booked rice. So the sale of rice trickled to a stop. This is story No.1.

Story No.2 goes like this. Zhang and I went to Hualian, a Beijing supermarket chain to see the manager and talk about the first story. The manager surfed the Internet and read the news about our rice and gave permission for Nanmazhuang rice to be sold in Hualian supermarkets. At that time in 2006, they had six stores. So on March 5, 2006, the stores began selling our rice.

[Professor He Huili, the Rice Professor from China Agriculture University]

These sales also began to taper off. Why? They did not allow our rice to get preferential treatment nor give us the proper documents to sell produce in supermarkets. Hualian allowed the sale of our rice only so they could take advantage of our fresh approach to rice. And when media stopped paying attention, so did they. The sales plummeted.

The supermarket also had fees we had to pay, for permission to sell at the supermarket. Although at the beginning the manager promised that we wouldn't have to pay certain fees, there were plenty of other ones. It also had standards that farmers could not meet, such as delivery and accounting deadlines, because Nanmazhuang was too far away. We gave up selling rice in supermarkets. As far as I know, the supermarket still owes the farmers 10-20,000 yuan for produce that is still in dispute.

Farmers don't like to take risks; they just want to gain profit in the short term. They cannot wait to be paid for their produce. They must have cash right away. Supermarkets, on the other hand, have a fixed date to pay producers and that date is often delayed.

After our sale of rice to Hualian, the government began to issue some policies to encourage supermarkets to sell organic produce. We were pioneers, so we had to bear such hardships, but other people were able to use our experience to get organic produce into supermarkets and sell healthier food.

But I don't want to sell rice; I want to create new institutions for the rural poor.

The 3rd story is our present plan to persuade Beijingers and organizations to prepay for the rice. Since supermarket sales after 2006 were not good, I realized that the only way to be successful was to create a marketing system for these contract sales. If we can contract the land out, then the farmers feel secure and will produce the better rice. A household needs at least 1/2 mu (1 mu is 6 acres.) of rice annually. For this they should pay 100 yuan. I was able to persuade many, many Beijingers and in the end 79 residents bought rice this way. This was the method for small-scale farming of organic rice and produce that villagers could handle.

A professor at Tsinghua University contacted all his friends to come out and buy rice. Beijing media, wanting to report on the reality of food safety, also supported us. One organization booked 100 mu and another booked 10mu and the rest were residents. In the end, it came to 150mu of land. *(Smiles – I can see she has been drumming up such support for years.)*

We did many, many activities to book rice. We had a National Day trip to Nanmazhuang in 2006 when 23 Beijingers went to the village to experience home-stay tourism. They visited farmer families, participated in talks about Nanmazhuang and visited the fields. It was successful because many Henan journalists covered the event.

We created another trip to the village when the rice was harvested. I invited professors, city activists and consumer representatives to talk together with the village producers. The real price of organic rice depends on three things: the market price, which is decided by the market supply and demand; the cost of soil recovery; and the profit that would encourage farmers to grow more organic produce. With the help of such experts, representatives of both producers and consumers better understood the structure of pricing and fixed the price using modern sustainable pricing formulas. The meeting is famous because so many journalists reported about it.

I have set up many urban-rural cooperatives throughout Lankao County. The farmers promised to plant organic food, and the consumer representatives promised to help market and disseminate information on behalf of the producers.

I had already created a cooperative at Beijing Forestry University. So we too, participated. We opened a store and sold produce from six coops there, all from Lankao County. The store earned 20,000 yuan. It was really a tea shop, so we didn't have to pay rent. The manager of the tea store just used the publicity we produced to help sell his tea.

Tsinghua University, Renmin University of China, China Agriculture University, and the China Social Research Institute – all of these intellectuals – liked the idea of getting Beijingers to care more about their food. After all, there were so many consumers in Beijing. But even though the media told

[Professor He Huili, the Rice Professor from China Agriculture University]

our story many, many, times, there was no long-term management concept or marketing plan, and sales dropped.

After we closed it, I used the 20,000 yuan to buy stock in Little Donkey Farm. This amounted to two shares. I also had three more shares from partners and friends. Little Donkey Farm is registered with the Community Supported Agriculture association. Today it sells Nanmazhuang rice in its store. So people know Little Donkey Farm supports our products and members and visitors can our rice there. The time is better now.

Nanmazhuang's Co-ops

He: The first goals of Nanmazhuang's urban-rural co-op were to cooperate with the urban co-op groups and to produce as organically as possible. Until now we haven't reached even the first goal. None of the cooperatives at the local level is working very well. Each has its own internal problems. I set up senior citizens and culture cooperatives and none has shown much success either.

Such co-ops have to survive in a capitalist society, which is more individualistic in nature, and this is not easy. On the other hand, rice is a commodity. This has monetary value. If the rice gets sold, the culture of the village gets better, and the senior citizens are more provided for. The three are linked to the same destiny.

But at present the market system is not right for selling our rice because everyone produces rice. With such low profit margins, there isn't enough surplus for themselves. The economic benefit is so low that the cooperatives don't feel that their collective efforts are worth very much.

I thought we could control the choice of seeds and manage the marketing. This would enable our brand to be sold in Beijing. My job was to help tell consumers and the rest of society that the influence of farmer cooperatives is important to food safety. So these farmers would earn more. We were not successful.

I tried to get Beijingers to care and that didn't work. I went to Lankao so residents there could learn to care about safe food and support organic farming. Nothing seemed to work the way we planned, but now things all are looking up.

Today days the ecological co-op has branched out and raises "happy pigs." Happy pigs are raised with no chemicals or hormones. They eat vegetable scraps, corn and cuttings. They are treated well.

Although these farmers have had their ups and downs selling the meat, the pre-paid contracts are on the increase, and the program is developing. The local government has provided winter pens for them. Recent pork-tainting scandals has been a source of benefit for Nanmazhuang farmers.

Also Zhang Yanbin, the mayor, recently made a deal with a car company who will be giving away Nanmazhuang rice as New Year's gifts and as end-of-sale gifts. It seems that all the learning by doing is creating new dividends.

Using Culture to Woo Sales

He: Before 2004-5 I did a lot to build up the cultural image of Lankao County. I believe that cultural development needs to match ecological development so that the economic system matures. I brought local singers to Beijing to perform. A series of cultural activities was staged at China Agriculture University to support Lankao cultural cooperatives – groups singing, dancing, playing drums. But it was too early, so the time was not right.

In 2005 we created a performance in Tiananmen Square. We printed a banner saying "People from Lankao show their respect to the residents of the capital!" which represented our deep desire for friendship and our willingness to provide healthy food for all the residents of Beijing. We also gave out bags of rice we brought with us to the Flag Honor Guard since they represent the capital.

[Professor He Huili, the Rice Professor from China Agriculture University]

Beijing journalists covered this but focused on the idea that a professor was leading this activity. They said nothing about the importance of safe food or the need for a healthy ecosystem. Again, this was not yet the time.

Throughout Lankao County, villages grow different specialties. In Chenzai they grow grapes. In Huzai, it is peanut oil and carrots. Since rice is the basic food, Nanmazhuang rice was always the most important product. This is why Beijing journalists were most concerned about the rice and the rice professor.

Beijing has organic stores now, and supermarkets that sell organic products. It has cooperatives and farms where they grow organic products in the area. Some are owned by foreigners, others by corporations, and a few individual farmers. Some are more seriously organic than others. Many now deliver to your door. Everyone knows the capital is a model for the whole country. Still, many consumers don't want to sacrifice quantity for quality.

He Huili participates in a cultural event in a village.

How to Make a Real Difference

Stephanie: How can real change take place for villagers?

He: After the reform and opening up was launched in 1978, Chinese villages were brought into the market economy. Labor, capital, and resources from villages flowed out to the cities and their own village integrity, both materially and spiritually, began to break down. However, no matter how China changes, it cannot survive without the villages. Now these villages are suffering from both internal distrust and mistrust of city people. A new cultural consciousness in rural areas, a new *raison d'etre*, has yet to develop. Without a respected role in Chinese society, farmers will only search for a way to make a profit for themselves. This is a problem for farmers but also for the urban residents who depend on them for food. We must find the right and respected place in modern China for them.

According to Liang Shuming's guidance, to do this, a new cultural self-consciousness needs to connect deeply with the culture and spirit of the villagers. The deep relationships, the belief in traditional principles for living wisely, must be part of this new equation. Urban residents also must awaken and respect the work and lifestyle of farmers as well.

The reform and opening up policy was initiated by Deng Xiaoping in 1978. It reversed the previous closed-door policy towards the world, allowing for economic development through private enterprise. This improved the living standards of many city dwellers. It also awakened a new way of thinking in the minds of the people, encouraging a diversity of ideas. However, farmers could not keep up with the market and lost ground to processed and industrialized agriculture.

He: In March 2011, I was selected to be vice mayor of Kaifeng, which is just a title, with no specific responsibility. Now, I can scale up my work and not just help Lankao, but also other counties in Kaifeng as well. At the same time, I will continue to support this vital awakening that still must take place.

[Professor He Huili, the Rice Professor from China Agriculture University]

Discussing urban/rural problems on the train to Kaifeng

Meeting with the Women's Federation in Kaifeng

We can learn something from how the Red Army developed its relationship with the farmers, which was to work, eat and live together with them but refuse to take anything from them. *(Armies in the past had always ravaged the farms.)* We had a better way to doing things back then like "borrow the wind" (to know when your own knowledge is not enough) and "to borrow the prevailing wind" (change strategies according to facts on the ground). The army gathered the support of the peasants. It was an effective plan of action. We need to think from the point of view of others. Then we can see how to move forward.

Everyone needs to consider what the villagers want, instead of telling them what to do to become successful. This is the start of good communication.

For example, my students at CAU and researchers at Henan University needed to find places to do fieldwork during summer vacations. Leaders of villages always ask me to invite such students. We have had some 50 students working in Yuanlou, Sanshi, Woshen and Zhanzhuang villages.

Research is the basic work of county-village cooperation. It needs to "start from what the villagers know, and be about how to help change what they have," James Yen said.

What do farmers know? What do they have? These answers should be in the research. Every morning, under my direction, students do research with family members in the village. They observe the local governance, ecological resources, market system, social ethics and cultural beliefs.

Since the research of the objects are human beings we should respect their feelings and ways of thinking. Especially since they are the most disadvantaged group in society, researchers have to double their respect and goodwill first. Then the farmers will be more willing to take part in the research and not be so reticent.

How can inexperienced young volunteers do this job well? When intellectuals want to help villages, they have to remember three things. I call them the Critical Triangle, and they are all centered on the common goal of awakening the villagers. Collaborative research. Get support of the county. Increase personal development. The main focus needs to be to dig out the cultural value of villagers and to develop it through county-village cooperation. This is what I teach students.

My experience shows that college students can have an important influence on the development of the village transformation process, if they add traditional cultural elements into their teaching, and emphasize traditional knowledge as much as possible. For example, students can tell their stories and histories through documentaries or share Chinese traditional adages (*three character concepts that teach a principle*) on how to live wisely. *Create Harmony in Community*, or *Create the Right Teacher-Student Relationship*, are good examples of Chinese traditional wisdom.

My students participate in setting up local cultural teams, work on re-establishing relationships between people by encouraging them to join in sports and cultural activities, such as aerobics, Yangsheng exercise (*local aerobics*), and Fengshou Yangge (*a rural folk dance*), and so on. Afternoons are the best time for studying together. Evenings are the time for exercise or cultural activities.

Successful research comes from good county-village cooperation. Successful cooperation happens because there are activist researchers who can influence and lead. In addition, our own self-development is important. It is the key and the power behind the research. It includes the capability of seeing the whole and being an example through your behavior in daily life.

In the market economy, everything becomes motivated by the desire for money. This has damaged the morality in counties and villages. So what is

[Professor He Huili, the Rice Professor from China Agriculture University]
129

the core task of county-village cooperation? The answer is to build moral fiber in the people from the cities (the researchers) at the same time.

But how can we do that? Before asking others to do something, we must do it first. For example, when it comes to the cooking for the team, the teacher needs to cook for everybody first; then the students will follow this example. In this way, the cooking problem is solved.

And when it comes time to clean, the teacher picks up trash and sorts it first. The students will follow the teacher's example. The kids will follow the students. Then the kid's mom and grandmother *(the men are all out in the cities working in factories)* will also clean and sort trash properly. This is the key to motivating people.

Volunteers should always remember what Dr. Wen Tiejun said, *"the right inter-cultural relationship* is the root to the revitalization of these counties and villages;" remember to use the "Critical Triangle" with a soft heart and you will see success. Revitalization will occur.

Stephanie: What continues to motivate you?

He: My basic work is good because it is both educating and taking action at the same time and place. This is my mission as a teacher: to arouse in my students the desire and ideas to realize the importance of a sustainable way of living for themselves and for fellow citizens. To create the soil to make my ideas grow. I tell them that creating a consciousness about sustainable living can be a good career if they are patient. Teaching is the most fundamental way to see progress.

This is what I do. I have my own students. I also have other students from groups around Beijing who ask me to teach them about organic and sustainable topics. So I get to teach a wide variety of young people. I also lecture at other universities and let everyone know how important these issues are. I tell my students that I am 40 years old and you are young. If one day my physical condition doesn't allow me to do this job, you can continue to do it. This is good for you and also for your family.

Connected with this is my desire to help organic farms around Beijing such as Little Donkey Farm and God's Green Garden. Two days ago I brought Kaifeng entrepreneurs to Ms. Zhang's farm. She and I are good friends. She has many worries so I want to help her. One of my students is there and will work for her for two months.

Zhang Zhimin is real. She understands the *dao* of agriculture and farming – but organics as a business is the norm. Agriculture is life but it is not a business. Beijing has Zhang so people can know about this. Zhang is doing very badly. Her prices are not right. They are too cheap. She is pure organic – she won't do business with people who are just concerned about price and quantity. Three years ago her membership fee was 1,000 yuan. Today the price is the same. There is something here that is not in balance.

Now I have another new development. My university dean has asked me to ask my contacts in Kaifeng for permission to send professors or students to do research there. I will not only be working with Nanmazhuang but also with other places. Kaifeng has 2,800 villages and five counties, only one of which is Lankao. I have not decided exactly how to do this, but this is another way to have impact.

One of my students, Lv Xun, is vice chairman of CAU Masters Students Union. I want Lv Xun to become a model and lead students to build a platform so people can understand deeply about ecology and sustainable agriculture. Students should not just help, teach or work in the villages. They should have an idea about sustainable agriculture themselves and how to build it. Not just teach in the village for a few days and then go away, but to really have an idea and pursue it until farmers really understand it and want to do it. Then they can work together to raise consciousness and build public awareness. To multiply the level of consciousness in our society.

A Sustainable Society

Stephanie: A sustainable society means one where people experience well-being, cooperate with one another, are happy about their lives, have mean-

ingful livelihoods, and sustainable consumers. Such a society, its politics and economy, is not GDP-centered but rather concentrates on the development of community.

A green economy only lengthens the time when resources will be depleted, the concept of a sustainable society makes more sense. We all need to learn to be sustainable. To cooperate with the rest of our "village," to better the "village." We all need to be in touch with the world but possess what we need. We are careful about our consumption at home and at work. We are conscious about our health and food. We are strong. But if we do get sick, we have good medical clinics. The schools for our children are good and connected with the world as well. Parents are at home and have good livelihoods that both enrich a sense of wellbeing and enable them to give back to the rest of the community. We all can live like this – the rural village and our urban community.[1]

I think the model of a sustainable society is perhaps something more attractive to villages in China. It is close to their traditional thinking. What do you think?

He: This is what we need to do for the villages. To bring together the traditional wisdom of the farmers and an economy that is win-win. This is how it used to be. This is how they feel deep inside. This is where we need to go.

Those who farm, will farm organically. They will be able to bring their produce to markets where they get the right price for their work – the right social, environmental and economical cost for growing that food. Because they care for their produce, they make sure that the bio-productivity of the soil increases. They get a good price and so are happy to grow the best, most nutritious food for their customers. They are respected members of the nation. They are interested in being more, not in having more.

Beijing's Impact on China

Stephanie: Beijing, as the capital, is seen as the model in China. Getting Beijing to join the growing international sustainable agricultural community is critical but to do that the residents have to trust the food.

He: I don't have a good impression of Beijing right now. Now Beijing is a cancer, so it needs to stop being a cancer. Beijingers realize that their city is not suitable to live in. So they drive out to the outskirts of Beijing for fresh air. I want to make Beijing a model for other big cities. To develop more organic farms, like Little Donkey Farm – to connect the downtown with nature and with natural agriculture. My job is to discover people who have ability who can work together with the rural farming community.

When I was younger I devoted myself to building institutions that strength-

The new organic supermarket in Zhengzhou

[Professor He Huili, the Rice Professor from China Agriculture University]

ened internal relationships. Now I want to give attention to find and train young people to help build the infrastructure for sustainable agriculture on into the future. Ecosystem education is also important in training. Institutions must be grown on good soil, and right now the urban/rural cooperation soil is poor.

However, we must continue to improve it. In 2010, together with Dr. Wen Tiejun and Zhang Yanbin, of Nanmazhuang, using our joint experience selling in Beijing, we came up with the idea to create an organic supermarket in Henan. In August and September we worked together with entrepreneurs and consumer co-ops. One of these is Lehe Shenghuo (the Green Consumer Coop). Its director is a member of Nature's Friend and he has been advocating sustainable living for quite some time.

In October 2011 we created the Guoren Supermarket in a two-story building in a busy part of Zhengzhou, the capital of Henan. The second floor is our Henan Guoren Rural/Urban Cooperative Service Center. It is where we have workshops for consumers, for students, and where the Henan Guoren Green Producer Cooperatives meet. These groups will work together to create the market. The supermarket, Guoren, will sell organic produce from different villages in the local area. Now we can encourage collaboration among the local villages and build the market.

What I have learned from my work in Beijing now helps me as Henan develops. The consumer co-ops in Henan were some of the first to start to prepay rice. In 2009 together we held the first organic cultural festival in Nanmazhuang. In 2010 these local consumer coops started booking organic pork. I have continued to educate and work with consumer co-ops in Henan ever since. And now we have the new organic supermarket in Zhengzhou open.

In December there was a large gathering of students from the local universities, co-op members, and some new consumers all there to learn about food safety and how to help people learn to value nutritious food. It was all arranged by the co-manager of the store, a woman in her early 20s. She is in charge of developing consumers. The students were excited and serious about being part of the change that needs to happen. The new consumers bought food. The co-op members are now exploring ways to connect to kindergartens so they can serve good food. A sustainable society is a long way away from reality for the moment. But the journey has begun.

Wang Zhiqin, Taiji Rouliqiu Teacher,
Connected to Nature, Naturally

Wang Zhiqin is my teacher. I learn Taiji Rouliqiu (Taiji Soft Ball) from her. Taiji Rouliqiu is pronounced Tiegee Roeleecho. This is a modern form of taiji that includes using a small racket to keep a ball in play. It has both the gentle and rhythmic moves of taiji and the eye-hand-ball coordination of modern sports. It exercises different muscle and joint combinations as well as enables the right brain to be balanced with the left. I had had some lung inflammation and this helped me heal. It also keeps me toned up. Many people have said that it has helped them cure illnesses, both physical ones like shoulder, back and joint problems and mental ones like depression. Most people say they have experienced weight loss and physical toning.

We both live at Fenglin Luzhou, an established apartment compound, near the Olympic Park, on the north side of Beijing. The compound is several salmon-colored apartments that surround or shape the garden complex. About half of the residents are retirees from the Academy of Sciences, which is just across the street. There are plenty of activities at the compound: different kinds of group exercises in the morning, individuals getting in their daily runs, grandparents taking care of grandchildren. And in the evening many people come out with their children, who bike and play while parents talk.

Taiji Rouliqiu is one of the morning groups. We always exercise outside except in the coldest part of winter. We are surrounded by the gardens. Wang is a fantastic teacher, always friendly, never critical and through her gentleness and patience, I have learned a lot about teaching, and Chinese ways of thinking and being.

Wang Zhiqin in red, third from the right

My body has benefited as well. She is a good example of the benefits of learning this new sport. She teaches me by basically demonstrating the movements because my Chinese is poor. We communicate telepathically because I really want to learn and she really loves to teach.

*****

Wang Zhiqin: I first found out about Taiji Rouliqiu in 2005. I retired in 2001 but didn't do a lot of sports. I became fat and had high blood pressure. It was time for me to do more exercise. One of my colleagues recommended that I learn this game. I felt much better after I did.

There was a group of people who played Taiji Rouliqiu at the Academy of Science. Xi Xiuzhen taught me to play the game. I didn't know her before. She was patient and enthusiastic. Later we played by ourselves here on the compound. Then some other residents saw us playing and joined in.

Taiji Rouliqiu was invented in 1991, by Bai Rong and his colleagues at Jinzhong Sanitation School in Shanxi Province. He was a boxing teacher. Every day before class the boxing teachers would fill the inner liner of the boxing glove with water and then fix it back into the glove. This was so the students would not get hurt during practice. One day, in fun, one of his colleagues threw him a liner full of water, and he used a basin in his right hand to receive it. When the liner touched the basin, he naturally moved the basin in a curve according the movement of the liner, and then swung it out of the basin into his other hand.

This fancy movement interested him very much. He practiced over and over and then improved on it by adding the ball and racket. Bai Rong had lots of background knowledge in Taijiquan. He found these two activities were very much alike in their core concepts, so he added the word "Taiji" to its name. In this way Taiji Rouliqiu was invented.

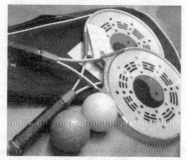

It combines the characteristics of Taiji-

Rouliqiu rackets and balls

quan, tennis and badminton. It shares the movements and principles of Taijiquan, which gives it grace and elegance. Rackets have a rubber film with a diagram of Taiji instead of netting, and the ball is the size of a tennis ball and filled with sand. The sand makes it easy to retrieve. Taiji Soft Ball is the only sport which is characterized by striking the ball indirectly. It has three basic movements: receiving, leading and throwing. The sport focuses on harmony and cooperative thinking.[1]

Her Background

Wang: When I was in high school, I was on the professional swimming team in my city. At my university, I played basketball. I was confident that I could do Taiji Rouliqiu very well. I think that it is a very suitable game for older people and it accords with Chinese traditional thinking.

My hometown is in Wuxi, Jiangsu Province. I graduated from a university in 1968, during the Cultural Revolution. At first I was sent to Henan Province and worked there for nearly 20 years, at a thermal power plant near Pingding Mountain. The place is famous of its coal reserves. Then I went to Beijing, where I worked as an engineer at the Institute of Electronics, at the Chinese Academy of Science across the street, until my retirement. The employees there are from universities from all over the country.

After the four perpetrators of the Cultural Revolution, known as the Gang of Four, were imprisoned, and normal society returned to China, my husband was admitted to the graduate school of the Academy of Science. He was sent abroad for four years to attend Cambridge University and Oxford University in the U.K. He came back to China in 1985 and began work at the Academy of Science. So that is when I came to Beijing. We have a son. He graduated recently from Beijing University and he is now a vice president at the Baidu Company, China's largest search engine.

The Gang of Four, four Communist Party officials, were responsible, in large part, for the Cultural Revolution 1966-76. Mao Zedong's last wife, Jiang

Qing, was the leader. They were all arrested in 1976, a month after Mao's death, and remained imprisoned until their deaths.

Wang: This apartment compound, Fenglin Luzhou, once belonged to the China Academy of Science. Some portion of the apartments were given to the employees of the Academy of Science. The rest were sold to other people.

The Game

Wang: Taiji Rouliqiu uses the soft to overcome the hard. The game or exercise starts with Set 1, which is foundational. You learn to keep the ball on the racket and develop the basic skills and techniques, such as twirling, having the ball leave the racket without force, back flips and from there do many interesting plays. These all must be done through the use of gentle and continuous connection between yourself and the ball. It seems to be weak, but it in fact the momentum also creates bursts of energy as well, without any additional force from you.

On the one hand, this game accords to the traditions of Chinese people. On the other hand, this game also has characteristics of Western sports. I really like Taiji Rouliqiu. I'm not so interested in Taijiquan because I think it is difficult and boring. When I play Rouliqiu, I use a racket to play but I use the soft to overcome the hard. It makes me feel more satisfied with why I am exercising to begin with.

It is different from other sports, where you hit the ball back directly with all your strength. Rouliqiu requires the players to receive the ball softly and then send it out still following the ball's pattern of movement.

This is a little like Taijiquan. When other people attack you, you receive the attack first. It seems weak, but in fact you can absorb the power and take advantage of the power to fight back. In short, when you are playing Taiji Rouliqiu, you must understand the ball's pattern of movement; otherwise, the ball will fall from your racket. The relationship between the ball and the player is different from other games. We use some physical principles, such as the centrifugal force, to control the ball. So many people say that the game requires sophisticated techniques and not everyone can learn it easily.

I think the most important thing is to understand the ball and take advantage of its power, just like our relationship with nature. We cannot violate the ball's pattern of movement. If we want to make the ball move according to our will, we must understand, respect it and make the right moves with our fingers, hands, arms and body so we are in accord with the ball's pattern of movement. We must move our racket at the ball's speed. Otherwise, the ball will leave the racket. In the same way, we must obey the laws of the nature first in order to take advantage of it.

The game makes you focus so you can put aside many unpleasant things. Before I began to play, I was depressed for a period, because my sister passed away. Then as I played the game with many other people, I found myself always talking with them and this made me feel better. In fact, everyone who plays the game feels happier.

I think the relationship between the player and the ball also has similarities with the relationship between me and other people. Just as the players must understand the ball's pattern of movement, a person must understand the characteristics of other people. We must understand people have different cultural backgrounds and personalities. We cannot force others to do something. Instead, we must understand first why he or she wants to do one thing or prefers another. We can cooperate better and achieve our common goals. I realized this after I learned to play. I became more patient.

The ball, even though it is made of plastic, is also part of nature. You want to make it stay on the racket. This represents a kind of stasis in nature. Humans and nature cannot live without one another. We don't merely seek harmony with the ball, we also need to make it move according to our own will. We don't just obey everything in nature. For example, to fight against droughts and floods is a kind of competition. We build dams and other facilities. This is a kind of competition with the nature. We have to change nature sometimes.

The Movements

If one performs Taiji Soft Ball as a single player, the play is to encircle the ball with the racket without interruption. The movements resemble and follow the principles of elementary Taiji. The ball is therefore held by skillful holistic body movements, internal focus and different flexible hand techniques. The movements can be choreographed to music as a dance form or with the movements of Taijiquan.[2]

Wang: As I said, Taiji Rouliqiu doesn't require direct hits and strong power. On the contrary, the concept of unifying contradictive forces requires players to receive balls positively and gently, to take advantage of the movement, and direct them naturally in a curve towards the direction we want the ball to go, using the inert centrifugal force to swing the balls away from us. The feature of the movement is soft not hard, smooth not angular.

On the other hand, the movements, coordinated by human body, racket and ball, reflect the concept of harmony of man with nature. A player should move his or her body, muscles, arms and legs naturally, making the body correspond with the mind. A good player is a part of nature, and when playing, cooperates with, not fights against, the natural power and laws of the universe.

So the best place to play is outdoors in parks or community grounds.

Daily Practice

Out at 8 in the morning, we are two rows of women. Some have one racket, others have graduated to two. Some start with one and then go to two. The music comes on with the instructor's voice for the first set. Later we graduate to just a lovely voice singing to us as we perform.

[Wang Zhiqin, Taiji Rouliqiu Teacher, Connected to Nature, Naturally]

Set 1: (warm up)

1. Swing the ball with one racket right and left for two counts of eight.
2. Swing the ball in a circle right to left for two counts of eight.
3. Swing the ball in a circle for two counts of eight stepping to the right and the left.
4. Swing the ball and turn 180 degrees to the left and then 180 degrees to the right.
5. Swing the ball 360 degrees to the left two times.
6. Swing the ball left and right letting the natural force of the ball release it into the air for eight counts.
7. Turn the racket and catch the ball, swinging right and left, each time you swing for eight counts.
8. Swing the ball in a circle right to left, releasing the ball at each swing and catching it for two counts of eight.
9. Swing the ball right and left and then under your left leg and then under your right one for four sets of eight.
10. Swing the ball right and left and then swing the racket behind you your back and release the ball and then capture it in front of you for four sets of eight.
11. Complete the set with two counts of eight swings.

Set 2: (to music)

1. Swing the ball to the right, twirl around the ball, to the left and twirl the ball and one more time to the left and then swing right and left to make the final five counts. Do twice.
2. Swing the ball to the right, twirl it around the ball and then swirl the ball over your head clockwise and then counter clockwise. Do twice.
3. Swing the ball to the right, and while your left arm moves counterclockwise, swirl the racket with the ball in a circle clockwise, then swing left and right, then twirl the ball towards your right and then turn around. Do the same set to get back to the front. Do twice.
4. Twirl the ball on your left and then turn full around counterclockwise twirl the ball around to the right and come back to center. Do twice.
5. Swing the racket and ball to the right, then do a circle and then release the ball and catch the ball, then twirl again and then release the ball again to the right, capture, and then swing right and left once more. Do twice.

6. Swing the ball right and left and then swing the racket behind your back and release the ball and then capture it in front. Then turn ¼ to the right and do it again, another ¼ and do it again, and one more ¼ until you are back in front. Then do two sets first in front and then in back for another two sets of eight.

7. Twirl the ball to the left and then make a small circle with the racket and ball, one way and then the other way and then for the final count turn around. Do the same and return to the front.

8. Complete the set doing two sets of eight swings making big circles in figure eights.

The other sets are more complicated. The third set is much more complicated, many more twirls, uses centrifugal forces to keep the ball from dropping as you spin around and it is almost perpendicular to the ground, and then with a partner, lobbying the ball (still using natural force) to one another either from under your legs or from behind your back.

Then you graduate to two rackets and learn to develop movements from both arms. I am now starting to do this and am amazed how much less flexible my left arm and wrist are. As I practice and get better, I can do a complete set, but clumsily. I also notice that my mind is clearer and I am getting more organized. Can my creative left be talking to my logical right? I even notice that I can now tell my right from my left. Is this the end of my learning disability?

The lady behind me, must be 10 years older than I, is always graceful, and completes her sets all with two rackets, with much dignity and poise.

As we practice, our neighbors come by. Their grandchildren with their mothers. Old friends. Young mothers with their very young children sit and watch us. Men play cards at the stone table near by. A father (during a holiday) teaches his daughter to rollerblade. It is our community. Everyone knows me now and for some reason is always happy to see me out there, and frequently give me a thumb's up.

At the end of each practice, my teacher and the graceful lady tell me how well I am doing, and how smart I am, and how quickly I have learned. My day is set and now I am ready for life.

[Wang Zhiqin, Taiji Rouliqiu Teacher, Connected to Nature, Naturally]

Understanding the Chinese Wisdom

Stephanie: What does it mean "Chinese traditional thought?"

Wang: Taiji Soft Ball is a kind of sport that emphasizes the harmonious relationship between human beings and nature, with the rest of humanity and between the body and the mind.

Though these concepts predate Chinese philosophy, the Chinese idiom "Tianren Heyi" (Man and Nature are One) characterizes the highest level of playing Taiji Rouliqiu. Human beings are an integral part of nature, according to Zhang Zai 张载 , (*the philosopher who created the idiom* "Tian Ren He Yi" *in the Song Dynasty (960-1279).*

Human beings are a component of heaven and earth, part of nature itself. Thus, the more human beings are in tune with the laws of nature, the happier they will be. Ethical principles are connected directly to natural laws. The ideal life for a human being is to attain harmony between yourself and the universe. To be in symbiosis. When we play Taiji Rouliqiu, we can attain better physical and mental health because we practice being part of nature, and recognize the need for this in our daily lives.

The idea of the Great Harmony is another ancient concept (see Introduction). It predates Confucianism and Taoism. A Grand Harmony, where all people coexist and flourish together. Grand Harmony (Datong) means the kind of harmony that unites people but respects their diversity. It is like a garden where there are many flowers and each contributes to the fragrance of the garden.

At the same time, the exercise or game is played with others. In Taiji Rouliqiu, we should seek out harmonies rather than generate conflicts. Everything is dialectic or resolvable through dialogue. The power that may seem feeble can contain great energy. Gentle movements can connect with the ball better than rough ones. Players can intertwine themselves with the movement of the ball.

In the same way, when playing with partners, and unifying the power within ourselves with that of our fellow players, we achieve "Wear away the rock with water" and can play well together.

Finally, Taiji Rouliqiu benefits our mental health because players must relax their bodies and purify their minds to play well. In this way the exercise seeks to rebalance the mental with the physical world. Players can sense their minds becoming stronger. They feel more confident and better about themselves. They see improvement in their mental agility as well as their physical health.

Of course, most people play for the enjoyment and don't think about all of this ancient Chinese wisdom. The game started long after the wisdom came down through the ages after all, so the wisdom is mostly unconscious.

Becoming a Teacher of Rouliqiu

Wang: When I was an engineer, I had responsibilities and the pressures of work. My colleagues and I had a working relationship at the factory or the Academy of Science. We had to finish our tasks. Sometimes I needed to cooperate with others and at others, finish the work myself.

Now I'm retired so there are no obligations and pressures. I can play Taiji Rouliqiu or teach others in the group totally according to my own desire and interests. Playing Taiji Rouliqiu is my hobby, and teaching others is just part of the hobby. Nobody is telling me what to do. I just do as I like. I'm in a free state.

There is another difference — people in the group at our compound come together because they want to. We all get along very well. When I was an engineer, my colleagues were already pre-assigned, not chosen by me. I *had* to get on well with them.

I changed from a manager to a teacher, but it is more than that. The change happened in my body and my spirit. Every morning, I go outside, breath the fresh air, stand under the sunshine, and do a gentle but toning exercise. It takes skill, so it is not boring and so keeps me interested. Gradually I found I'd feel bad if I didn't exercise outside. Moreover, I can be with people who are now my friends.

I still feel I do not play Taiji Rouliqiu well enough. I see others perform the same movements more gracefully. I was once an athlete. Although I'm good at gymnastics, I feel my movements are not graceful enough.

To do it well is very different from teaching others well. Some people can do it very well, but they are not good at teaching. I think I'm good at teaching, and this game has made me very patient.

I think there are two very important points to being a good teacher. First of all, a good teacher must know how to break down each movement and make people understand. Some people can set up simple examples for others, but they cannot make them understand. A good teacher must clearly explain the key points and the significant parts of the movements. It is also important to be able to explain the profound in simple terms.

Secondly, when students make mistakes or are not doing well, a good teacher must notice this instantly and point it out. A good teacher must let students know how to make progress.

This discernment about what to say and how to say it makes her a great teacher.

Wang: The qualitative change in my teaching happened gradually. I became aware of these points through my experience. When I teach others, I find people are willing to learn. I like thinking about why. So I gradually adjust my teaching method to help them even more.

My first teacher who showed me the world of Taiji Rouliqiu was not a very good teacher in fact. But she was a nice person, very kind and warm-hearted. I also learned many specific and some difficult sets from watching the DVD/VCDs with another older lady.

I also learned a lot on my own. No one can do every set well. Everybody has different abilities. Some people cannot catch on. My teachers were not always patient, and I didn't like that. So I didn't follow their example as a teacher.

When a new learner comes to the group, he or she can't learn just by watching and imitating. If there isn't someone to guide you, it will be very troublesome to learn. The game is very simple but deep.

Stephanie: Did you learn to teach from experience with your family?

I get on well with my son, daughter in law, my husband and others who help me around my home. My husband is not out-going. But my son is like me. People say my son has a broad mind and is kind. In many Chinese families, there are conflicts between a mother-in-law and the son's wife. But I get on well with my daughter-in-law. I try and think how to understand others more and why sometimes we have different opinions. Like with Rouliqiu, communication is important.

Wang Zhiqin is in the background.

I feel that it is very valuable for people to be outdoors and have the will to exercise, so I'm happy to teach them.

I want to help others if I can. I feel happy when people get involved in our group. Helping others is a kind of happiness. Some people may think that helping others people play well is not their business, but I'm not that kind of person.

Because of this sport, I know conflicts are unnecessary. It is unnecessary to confront the tough with toughness. We should first receive the force and send it back by the virtue of the ball's movement. When students and I can have different opinions, I will listen at first. But the one who obeys the rules of nature will be proved to be true in the end.

Stephanie: You know you never make me feel badly. You laugh when my ball falls, you cheer when I do better, or when I get something – and all of this is done in basic sign language.

Wang: I think it is natural. I'm inspired by your hard work. Balls fall, after all. (*laughs*)

Competitions

Wang: There are three kinds of Taiji Rouliqiu. One is to play by yourself. This can be very creative and graceful and a good way to exercise. Or you can play with a group, as we do, and do several fixed sets, each more difficult than the next. You can play with one or two rackets as well. We do this. Or you can play against someone with one or many balls in play.

In 2002, the Sports Association of Older Persons organized many groups all over the country to spread this sport. These days, the sport can be seen in communities, schools, parks and gyms.

The Chinese government is also very interested in promoting the sport. Taiji Rouliqiu (Taiji Soft Ball) is emerging as a national sport in China. The first national championship was in 2010. China has an aging population so keeping healthy and preventing diseases are encouraged. Rouliqiu is also being taught at the Physical Education University in Beijing. You can also study for a master's degree in Folk Physical Education there. Rouliqiu is also taught at Shaolin Temple and other places famous in martial arts history.

Wang: It has become popular also among young people. Some high schools and universities already provide it as an elective. In addition, different kinds of competitions and games are held in towns, cities and across the country every year, motivating people to improve themselves and work with other players.

Another kind is where players seriously compete with each other. There are two kinds of competition. The first kind is with a net and there are singles, doubles and mixed doubles games. The players have to pass the ball in a way that is very difficult for their opponent to receive it.

I once was a referee for such a competition in Beijing, with my teacher, Xi Xiuzhen, for the Set 1 level. Usually the competitions have both sets and performance contests. We studied the Rules of the Game and judged the plays accordingly. It was a city-level competition.

There are many judging requirements for such competitions. How the racket must be held, its angle during certain moves, dropped balls, or balls that disconnect from the racket.

The second kind of competition is to compete for best performance, as you would in a dance competition. You can compete as a group or individually. The ones who perform most beautifully win. There are many requirements for performances too, of course.

Our group has also performed and won prizes. At one time we formed a team as the Academy of Science and won. We divided into three teams of 20 each, so a group of 60. We attended the Beijing city-level competition three times and also another national performance.

Sometimes we represent an organization (such as the Academy of Science), and they pay for our uniforms and transportation. Sometimes we represent the community here, and our Homeowner's Association gives us money for uniforms and other materials. And then at other times, we all chip in and create our own uniform.

I remember in 2006 we performed together with 1,000 people at the grand finale! All of us doing this graceful dance of exercises together. It was wonderful to see.

There were teams from Japan, Germany, and England at Shijingshan Gym. It was for the Pagoda-Tree International Cup (named because the inventor's name, Bai Rong, means white pagoda-tree in Chinese).

We don't know how these people learned of the game, but they were very enthusiastic. They performed as soon as they arrived, so they must have been already practicing in their home countries. Now there are schools and competitions in these countries as well.

They didn't compete, of course. We showed new moves to them but they already knew how to do the basics. They performed with us in the grand finale.

There were even disabled people performing in wheelchairs. They performed but also played competitively.

Stephanie: You just started in 2005, but in 2006 you performed at an international competition?

Xi Xiuzhen: (*her teacher joined us for a talk, listening, and smiles proudly*) and says, "I taught her one on one. She is very good."

Wang: The inventor Bai Rong attended our performance too, by the way.

As a Social Event

Stephanie: I will tell you what amuses me. For me, when I play, I have to concentrate hard. Up and down, up and down… but everybody else around me is chatting away, talking about this and that and yet swinging that racket without any balls falling on the ground. Talk, talk, talk… How do you do that? I cannot do that. I can't possibly do that! If I even think of something else, the ball falls.

Wang: (*Ha ha ha*)! Wang Laoshi laughs but, her teacher is not so pleased.

Stephanie: But I like it that you have a nice social group, it's great! I like it! How can you all be so good that you don't even have to think about it?

Wang: Because we have been playing the game for a long time. Everybody has different thoughts. Most of us are doing it for the fun and exercise. Most of us are old, so we don't care much about perfect form and such. As time goes by, people become so skilled that we can talk and play at the same time. At first even if we focused, the ball would fall. But now we do not focus and the ball doesn't fall.

Bai Rong was basically just a man of the people. He was a boxing teacher. In Beijing alone, there are about 100,000 people playing the game he invented.

I think it is so popular because you can build up your body and keep fit. It is part of their past but also modern too. It combines dance moves too. Others create gymnastic moves and sets for themselves.

People can create their own style. There is even an optional part of the competitions, as in gymnastic competitions. So it is very creative. It is very personal. It is the best activity for people. So many people love it.

You can't learn Rouliqiu using a DVD. You have to have a teacher. It best spreads one to one. Some go to the parks to find others who practice. Or find someone in their apartment compound to learn from, or from colleagues at academic or research institutions. Now 2 million people around the world have found out about it. There is even an American website.

Friends

Wang: I am interested in what you are doing here in China. I know your work in Henan. I used to work down there. You are helping a village that is trying to develop organic produce and market it, right? We already have some organic food in supermarkets here, but consumers are not sure whether what they buy is really organic. For example some so-called organic pork was found to be just normal pork. You know, in Chinese society, there is a lot of fraud.

Stephanie: Not just in China. We need smart consumers. Educating yourself is critical. Women have an important role to play. If you educate yourself, then you can make good choices. If more and more people make the right choices, the whole market will change.

[Wang Zhiqin, Taiji Rouliqiu Teacher, Connected to Nature, Naturally]

Wang: You devote yourself to environmental protection at your age, and I admire you very much. I'm about the same age as you, but I just do exercise for others. I think your spirit is very admirable.

Stephanie: I'm always in admiration of you. I talk about you to everybody. (We smile at each other.) I am a teacher of dialogue, but I have learned how to dialogue better from you. I teach global citizenship, but I teach it better because I feel like my body is more a part of the universe.

Now when I come out here in the morning, I can feel the trees. I can feel them. I feel the presence of the flowers.

One of our ladies must have been a dancer. She dances her Rouliqiu, silently and gracefully, attuning her inner self with the energy of the life around her – the sun, the air, the wind, the earth. Swirling the ball and racket, dancing, gliding, she is perfectly connected. She dances her own dance usually and then joins us for our practice every day. She is beautiful to watch.

Now I finally understand that Taiji Rouliqiu – when you are very skilled – becomes like your own private dance. My dance.

Wang: Yes.

Stephanie: You say it is creative. It is also very personal. It is my dance. My dance with nature.

Wang: Yes.

Therese Zhang Zhimin, Human Beings and Nature, and the Art of Agriculture

Zhang Zhimin is like *junzi* with the land. She is struggling to put back into the soil of Beijing, and therefore the soil of China, the deep cultural values the Chinese need and restore the inherent balance between humanity and nature. Listening to her is like being able to hear the soil of China speak. With tired patience, she expresses what is in her heart. Her farm is a member of the International Federation of Organic Agricultural Movements (IFOAM), is a CSA, and the first organic farm certified both in cultivating and animal feeding in China.

Zhang Zhimin and I

Zhang Zhimin giving an introduction to her farm to ECCN staff and graduate students

She picks me up in her battered car. We'll make a final delivery and then we head south to her farm.

She talks in a very quiet voice and tells her story with patience and doesn't mask the struggle it takes to give her whole life to the task she has set forth for herself. She doesn't care about the sacrifices. She wants to make a difference.

Today, I am her student. By the end of the interview, I have become a supporter, an admirer, and a novitiate seeing Chinese civilization from a different perspective – seeing agriculture for the first time from the perspective of human beings with nature. Come along for this ride!

*****

Zhang Zhimin: (*while driving*) A couple, part of my staff, just left a few days ago and so I've had to work without a full staff. The young man who delivers for me and I worked until 3 o'clock in the morning to prepare the produce this week. I have been working hard here for 10 years, so I can't stay up so late anymore. We then got up at 5 a.m. and began the packing.

We left the barn at 7:30 and then drove all day. It was 8 in the evening and we were still not done. So I told my final customer that I would deliver her produce in the morning. That is why we need to go there first before going to the farm.

I live in the north part of Beijing and Daxing, in the south, is where her last customer is. Her farm is further south in Jiang Village, Liangxiang, Fangshan District.

Zhang: The couple has just moved back to their hometown to buy an apartment. Even though they've been working here in Beijing, for me and for others, for 20 years they still cannot afford an apartment in Beijing. When they go to their village, they may not feel like they've come home because they've been absent for 20 years and nobody knows them anymore. The neighbors in the village will think they did not do well in Beijing. So they've decided to buy an apartment in the downtown area – near to the village but not in the village. They are familiar with the downtown and so they feel it is still home to them.

I am the only organic farm in the south. At the beginning when I asked some friends to help me look for land, we explored the Changping area, about 20km north from the capital but still in Huairou County. Huairou, really more to the east, was already developing as suburbs spread out. I thought that farmers would soon have to give up land in the north. I didn't like it that the land was so occupied. So I went south – because I'd be able to stay longer.

Stephanie: You have been proven right. Most of the land to the north now consists of apartment compounds.

Zhang: At that time I didn't think about marketing, (*laughing ruefully*), I just wanted to practice farming the right way. I didn't know much about agriculture at the time either, but my idea was to start a farm, practice the traditional way as much as possible and cooperate with nature.

I've an export marketing background of 20 years – canned goods and agricultural products. In 1985, I learned the word "residues" and felt strange that there were regulations approving them in many countries. From this I knew we had some problems in our food supply. I wanted to find a way to get healthier food for my family and me. Supermarkets had been developing since the early 90s, but although I was hungry but I couldn't find much to eat in these stores. I felt empty and thought to myself: I want a farm one day after I retire. It became my dream.

In 1997 China signed an agreement with the U.S. to permit imports, which was to start in three years. In 2000 I began a new business, the import of American fruits. Unfortunately, it was impacted by the process of China entering the WTO. Through the struggle of losing this business, I suddenly felt a mission to do agriculture. I really wanted to find a way for farmers to grow the right food and to make a better living.

I found a piece of land, 150 mu (10 hectares) in early 2001 and started to build my farm. At that time I wasn't living on the farm. I would give the work to the farmers only to discover when I visited that nothing was done right. They didn't really take any responsibility. So I moved onto the farm itself. How did they lose such care for the land? I began to explore this problem.

Culture Revolution Experience

Zhang: When I was a child during the Cultural Revolution, I went to the countryside a lot. I asked people why I saw so few villagers working in the fields. I learned some of the reasons. The farmers refused to work because food prices were unreasonably low so that everyone could eat – everyone except for the farmers. They decided to stay away at harvest times.

At the end of the Cultural Revolution, the government gave small pieces of land to each family and this changed the situation. The farmers were then trained in industrial agriculture, learning much of this from the West. So the farmers' attitude changed. They no longer wanted to work so hard. They had land but why should they work hard when the price of food was still so low that they couldn't make a good living?

"Why won't they work?" I asked myself. To be a farmer used to mean being honest and hardworking. Why did they change so much? They were not being reasonably paid. Also, industrial agriculture enabled them to produce with less work. The connection between the land and the farmer was broken.

The problem worsened as the land on conventional farms became less able to sustain crops. Farmers had to add more and more fertilizer to the land as well as pesticides because of monocropping. Everyone became more and more distant from a land that was once kept fertile through traditional wisdom and methods.

Her Ten-Year Struggle to Create Connections

Zhang: People want to buy the cheapest produce but farmers can't live on prices like these. Farmers are just getting over the Cultural Revolution – and aren't we all? Unfortunately, today our society has many interests and caring for others is a low priority.

We just celebrated the Dragon Boat Festival. We celebrate it each year around June, according to the lunar calendar, the 5th day of the 5th month. It commemorates a famous statesman during the State of Chu, Qu Yuan, (339-278 BCE). He was a very famous poet as well. He was banished because he opposed an alliance with the Qin that his king decided to accept. Later, the Qin conquered the State of Chu, and Qu Yuan in despair threw himself into the river. The local people, who admired him, dropped rice wrapped with bamboo leafs (*zongzi*) to prevent the fish from eating Qu Yuan's body. These zongzi are eaten today to pay respect to Qu Yuan and the common people back then.

"Deeply sighing, weeping and crying, I feel sad for the hard life of common people," one of his poems goes. *"The road is too far to go* (she is weeping now) *but I will continue seeking, far and wide, along it."*

I learned this poem in primary school. I think about a man like that. If we have a history of 5,000 years, we should be more civilized and wise. I feel very sad.

The life of farmers is always hard. Hard life can make people difficult. When I was first at the farm, the farmers were so hard on me, and it hurt me because I was trying so hard to help them. The poet thought and felt deeply about the people, so much so he jumped into the river. But I can't, for there is no longer a river nearby, and because I will continue – and I still believe that I can find my strength in the values of my civilization.

Stephanie: So how are you rebuilding the connection with the soil?

Zhang: At God's Grace Garden, we practice the principle of diversity and rotate our crops. We arrange our work following the rhythm of nature.

We prepare compost on our own, and have several compost places. These are our "kitchens," where we prepare food for our soil. We are a biodynamic farm with Chinese characteristics. (*smiles*)

In ancient times, say 1,500 years ago, pest control was not an important activity in farming. We farm the same way. We let the weeds grow and we harvest them with gratitude. The weeds give nutrients to animals, plants and to our soil.

I've learned to listen to the land. I also read ancient texts and try to apply their wisdom to my needs. It is a continuous learning process. The soil has become increasingly more fertile. If you look at the soil on my farm, you will see it is rich with a diversity of plants. The soil is full of gifts, of earthworms. Our soil will feed people. The produce of such soil cannot be just merchandise. When food becomes a commodity, the safety of food is at risk.

We sell our produce through memberships. By signing up to be GGG Organic Agriculture Club members, you are voting with your food budget to protect our ecosystem, support organic farming and recreate a healthy environment as well. A deposit of 1,000 yuan will hold your share and will be applied to your purchases.

We only have a few members now. I believe in letting people decide what they want to eat, what they ask of the soil. However, most people cannot distinguish the difference between this farm and that farm, because their connection with the soil is so distant.

Today the consumers do not know the value of what they are buying. Some people are angry when they find insects in their grain because they don't know that pesticides are used to store grain as well as to grow it. Other people refuse to buy vegetables if they are not as soft as those grown in greenhouses. They don't know greenhouse vegetable production wastes much more water, stresses nature, and even troubles the function of the ecosystem. They don't understand that naturally grown vegetables need more support to keep pace with the change of climate, and still be more nutritious. Much to my regret, sometimes I hear people say: "If again I find some insects in your grain and vegetables, I won't buy anything from you and I'll tell all my friends not to buy from you."

People are unaware of the social and environmental costs of organic farming. I have a very good education and my friends are wealthy people. But even they said it was too expensive when I started the club. Once a lady only bought one jin of vegetables even though I drove 60 km to get to her home. Delivery was free at that time. Such experiences disappoint me very much.

Local farmers or native farmers have free land, but I'm not a native farmer, I have to pay for the land, and I have to pay salaries plus oil and gas for the car. At the same time, there are few experienced workers. I have to train local workers and pay them. The local farmers don't want to learn, so they don't stay.

Few members want to work in the fields. Still some consumers, before they make the decision to buy organic food, ask me to assure them of the air and underground water quality. How can I do that? To be an organic farmer, you have to feed the soil properly, to train people freely, to offer home delivery, to feed people with safe food, to do whatever the consumer-gods want, to work day and night but without any income.

I'd like to ask these consumer-gods, why does someone like me, without even a social insurance card, take on so much social and ecological responsibilities? I am losing not only money, but my life.

[Therese Zhang Zhimin, Human Beings and Nature, and the Art of Agriculture]

I don't want to make money but I do want to provide a service and break even. I run from morning to night, I have fed the soil for more than 10 years in a biodynamic way. It makes a difference, but sales are low. When I send out my produce, I feel I am the bridge between urban citizens and the soil. I am the go-between. Unfortunately, not many are listening, or feel this connection deepening.

We are a whole community of relationships. We know we are an ecosystem, but only from a scientific point of view normally. But it is more than that. Life, the ecosystem, must work harmoniously.

Consumers need to realize what they owe these farmers who, for so many centuries, provided them with food. That is why I wanted to be a working farm, just like other farmers. I decline connections with businesses for this reason. I want my prices to be what a farmer would receive – for my farm to be a fair trade endeavor.

I am grateful to the members who are my friends. My problems make me understand what we face as a society. I want us to revert back to what people owe nature, what society owes its farmers, and government owes agriculture – if I pay this debt – every organic farmer will make money.

I hope I can change something. This is the smallest business I have had, but from the moment I started, I have felt I had a mission. It is the key. In this small way I can create a path. I may lose all my money but in other ways I gain a lot. Other people can't begin to understand how worthwhile it is. I am a woman and so I have a better way to understand what I am doing. It is like giving birth. So pain and hope are what I have. Miners take out the earth and millionaires have a lot of oil – but both are destroyers.

Stephanie: So farmers are the feeders of the nation? Something seems out of balance here.

Zhang: You are right. For example, the other day there was a forum on how ecological agriculturalists can make money. There was a general manager of an organic farm from Shanghai there. They call themselves organic but they just focus on vegetables. This is not truly organic. To be organic, you need a certain percentage of trees for coverage, and other things, like animals for manure, for the vegetables to grow organically.

You can't get organic vegetables by just investing 200 million yuan and growing vegetables. Vegetables only take a few days to grow. So why should they cost so much? From the 1,700 mu of land, they use only 1,100 mu for production. They have 6,000 customers in Shanghai and they want to market in Beijing and Guangzhou. In each city he said he wants to have 5% of the market. The man didn't mention his workers. Who are his workers? His workers are mostly women and their average age 57.

The point of the forum was how to make money. People don't know what organic culture is – they just use the word and don't realize that the standard for "organic" means that the whole farm has to be involved. That includes the human beings – the farmers. Farmers are collaborators with nature. Farming is the art of collaborating with nature. How well we cooperate with nature is subject to how well we know nature. How well we want to cooperate with nature. Farmers are feeders of the nation. Why shouldn't people who take responsibility for feeding others be paid reasonably for their work and be respected for what they do?

Her Farm

Coming through her gate onto the farm, I see it is a complete farm – sections for orchards, vegetables, cows, chickens, turkeys. Dogs galore. There are white signs with large Chinese characters and explanations. The farm has beds of flowers and crabapple trees in front of a long, white building. On the left are staff quarters, then a large room with tables for groups who come in to help or buy, and then her own quarters. It is a real farm.

Zhang: Here, this is my farm. It's called God's Grace Garden (天福园 *tian fu yuun*). One of the characters I put on this sign here is 福 (*fu*) meaning good fortune, blessing or happiness. When I am working on my farm, I am full of revelation.

A biodynamic farm

I like to muse about Chinese concepts that reveal our connection to nature, and decode their meaning. Look at this word. The left part is 示 (*shi*) means to present and to reveal. Many words composed with 示 are connected with the god. What does this word 福 (Chinese for good fortune) reveal to us? 一 口 田 . 一 for one, 口 for mouth and 田 for land. "One" means the heaven, the god who is on high. "Mouth" means to eat and live. To eat and live is a basic human right. "Land" means to work. To work is also a basic human right. Land also means the world. In the character 田 we can find many 口, which means many people, many livingbeings, so it means also a world. It is not good to be alone. When we have faith and food, when we work and work together we feel happy. This is the true meaning of this concept. It is like a revelation. It is truth.

When I work in the field, sometimes I prefer to work on my own and think. I play some word games to reveal the scope and meaning of my work – Chinese words are full of revelation. For example, the character for life: 生 (*life*) is composed of 人 (*human*) and 土 (*earth*). Here we have a person connected to the earth. We can interpret this as the relationship between humans and the earth.

Again the character for 食 (*food*) is composed of 人 (*human*) and 良 (*good*) and means that food is something good for humans, food is the foundation for human life. A Chinese proverb says, "People make food a god" (民以食 为天 *min yi shi wei tian*). It is not a fair deal if we exchange our labor for food that contains poison. At the same time, when we have a choice, we should choose healthy food.

The character for 胃 (*stomach*) is composed of 田 (*land*) 月 (肉 *meat*). Meat represents our physical body and so the stomach is the farm of our body. The stomach can digest, absorb, and provide nutrition. Just like the farm which digests, absorbs and provides nutrition as well. In Huangdi Neijing (*Yellow Emperor's Canon of Medicine*), a medical book from ancient China, it says that the stomach is responsible for the health of the blood. The nutrition in the blood comes from food, which comes from the real kind of farm. So when farms are healthy, people are healthy.

I don't want to do monoculture. To have a healthy farm is all about the soil – soil is a kind of land that can grow by itself and give seeds. What is soil? The Chinese character for soil is 壤. It is composed of 土 (*earth*), 衣 (*cloth*), 口 (*mouth*), 井 (*well*) and presents several ideas all in one concept that describes the value of soil.

It is earth plus the commodities that come from the earth, plus the idea that the soil produces food equally for both humans and all other creatures. This means that humans must be in harmony with others. *Water in the well* is also contained in this character. The value of the topsoil creates the right balance with the water for the plant to grow. The water is regulated by the well. Thus, the collaboration between human beings and the soil ensures the continued, or sustained, nourishment of human beings. We can get food through continual cultivation and good management. It is all made up of life. What I mean to say is that the soil is a resource for us all. But it is not endless. We must use it cooperatively with the rest of life and use it wisely. The soil will hold water – if it cannot, it will go away – like the loess plateau. If we lose too much water, the soil will blow away. As it is blowing away now.

In Chinese writing, the character for agriculture has now been simplified

The character for "soil"

[Therese Zhang Zhimin, Human Beings and Nature, and the Art of Agriculture]
163

as 农. Traditionally it was composed of *qu* (曲) and *chen* (辰). *Qu* (曲) means art, for example to prepare alcohol, some leavening or aspergillus needs to be worked together with grain. When we prepare it, we need to take into consideration the time, temperature, moisture and other data. It means we cannot prepare agriculture at just any time. You have to wait for the right time and right season.

This is the way to make good produce, good wine and good cheese. *Chen* (辰) is a general calling for the sun, moon and stars. Light is very important to plants, and farming activities must follow cosmic rhythms. So the word for agriculture is composed of *qu* (曲) and *chen* (辰) which means agriculture is the art of people with nature. That is why when we do agriculture, we have to respect nature, learn from it and work with it.

You will see that there are a number of signs on my farm with Chinese characters. These are to remind myself, and others, of the deep connection between humans and the soil.

My farm is not an artificially created ecosystem. It is not an ecological park for tourists. My farm is a self-sustainable ecosystem. Without this kind of ecosystem, you cannot have agriculture.

The land beneath us is local land. The nation feeds everyone, but local people have to feed the local land. Organic agriculture is a poem written by the human being about nature.

When we live in balance with the rest of life, we will have clouds in the right seasons, and they will give rain to all life. In Hebei, why is there to less and less rain? Because the forest has been lost. The earth was perfect. China created the Loess Plateau because of poor management of the soil in the past. We should learn from this mistake.

The Yellow River did not use to be yellow. And it didn't use to be so high. All of this, over thousands of years, is man-made destruction. What a nation does with its agriculture reflects what kind of civilization it is.

Here is another sign post. The message is from Guan Zhong (c.720-645

BCE): "If one man doesn't cooperate with the soil, there will be hunger, if one woman doesn't weave, there will be people without clothes."

Guan Zhong was part of a group known as the agronomists. Agricultural treatises by them have an important place among the "masters and philoso-phers" of China because of the crucial role agriculture played in the economy of traditional China.

Man and labor and land. This is the correct relationship with the land. Men working the land are both a social division of labor but also an ecological one. The land and many plants are female, so you need a man to work on them. Now women do the farming and men go out to work in factories. This is out of balance. The land needs more men working on it. We have many more boys than girls now but none of them wants to farm. Why is that?

If we want a better life, we need to work hard. We should be laborious – use our hands and bodies for the sake of the land and to our duty for our society. It is a shame that we don't think this way anymore. People only care about their own problems of poverty and not about the spirit of being human. We need to work efficiently to perform our duty to life. This is the high standard we need to meet again.

I believe that the ancient fathers of Chinese civilization felt deeply about the land around them. They didn't just use it. They connected with it. They collaborated with it. They harmonized with it.

Stephanie: I can feel, just walking around, that there is a cohesion here.

Zhang: Here are our cows, sheep and goats. Now they're having a rest but soon we will let them out to roam. Turkeys and chickens run free. The turkeys are new, but once they are get used to their surroundings, they will become the guardians of the chickens. All animals here are friendly. They are not afraid of us. The cows will stand up and make a connection with you if you are willing.

Walking by a flowering sapling, she stopped and admired it and then the row of paulownia trees that separate the fields from the rest of the farm.

Zhang: This is something I used to see as a child and happened to find such a tree again and so brought it to my farm. These (*pointing to the paulownia*) are local trees that line the road. They shed, so they are not liked much around here, but they are very good for the soil.

Plants that do not produce for you, still add value to the farm. They purify the air, or they add beauty or scent. Some of them may help with pest control. According to what plants I know, or discover, I use such plants to enrich the farm. Different plants have different capabilities.

Weeds tell us something too. In the ancient books, it says certain weeds will tell us what kinds of grains to plant. It is difficult to do this these days because people use too much herbicide. Because of climate change, people want to control everything and this impacts the functioning of the ecosystem. Human beings are not sensitive to the changes in the ecosystem. We need to discern what it is saying to us?

We also produce according to the market, of course. We need more wheat for flour, for example. We grow corn to feed the animals. We plant a lot of legumes and vegetables.

Weeds are a vital part of this ecosystem.

Her childhood memory has a home.

Reconnect to Nature

Listen to the soil, plants and insects. If we irrigate or sow at the wrong time, this is not in balance. It is not a very simple message. We have to listen deeply.

Stephanie: Insects?

Zhang: Insects die from the chemicals we use but you notice that they are still here.

We are so disconnected from nature. I remember that there once was a TV advertisement about *Laifuling* pesticide in the late 1980s. Some insects appeared on the screen first, then the pesticide arrived, with a song, "We kill pests, we kill pests... Just Laifuling, just Laifuling, we must kill the insects to death! To death! To death!"

This TV advertisement existed for quite a long period, and it influenced many people. It spread such information like, "Pesticide is right, so pesticide is a good thing."

Since the 1990s, the production and usage of pesticide have been increasing at an alarming rate. Agriculture has become a war between humans and insects. Before planting, farmers douse the land with pesticide. Then steep the seeds with pesticide. When the plants are ready to grow, they spray crops with pesticide again and again. After harvest, they use pesticide again. In order to preserve crops ready for market, they then mix powdered pesticide (whose main chemical composition is phoxim) and spray it on the products.

Some farmers have come up with their own usages. One of them is to prevent stealing as crops ripen. Since the farmers are too busy to watch the fields, and it is not safe or cheap to hire somebody to guard them, farmers will spray a great amount of pesticide on them. The would-be thieves know they will get sick, so they don't pick them. This is now the most economical, efficient and convenient way to prevent stealing.

[Therese Zhang Zhimin, Human Beings and Nature, and the Art of Agriculture]

Maybe it is because of the side effects of the pesticide that people don't seem to realize what this is doing to them. Or maybe it is because they think such poisons will not harm humans and animals. People don't seem to realize that pesticides do matter to human health.

Normally putting poison onto another's plate would be considered a crime. However, spraying poison on food that goes on your plate is somehow "proper" behavior. If someone tries to put poison onto your plate, you would not let him. But people do nothing even when they know someone has put poison into the food before they eat it.

Agricultural civilization has a history of nearly 10,000 years, while chemical agriculture only has a history of about 100 years. Since people have changed the way the farmers do farming, "pest" damage has become more and more frequent. Killing and preventing the pests have become an important part of agriculture. There are more and more new kinds of pesticides, but the "pest" damage is increasing. A war has begun between human and insects.

Many insects began life on the earth before humans appeared. We need them in ways we don't realize. Insects also have the right to life, and their lives are meaningful to us as well. For example, a cockchafer's (june beetle) life cycle corresponds with a tree's growth cycle. The beetle likes eating the buds of trees and young leaves.

This prevents the tree from being overcrowded and having too many branches and leaves. More light can shine on the trees, and this benefits the beetles because the tree will grow new buds. There is a peasants' proverb that says: "Trees won't grow fruits without light." Inspired by such cockchafer's behavior, people who are respectful can learn how to prune fruit trees.

In any art, skill and knowledge are important. In two weeks there will be many of these june beetles here. Some all black, others are red. The red is the male and the black is female. I found that when I take away the male then the black ones disappear and don't lay eggs. In this way the insects are controlled. Some will remain but that is okay. If you observe carefully you can understand how to act wisely.

Take aphids, for example. Farmers will see them on fruit trees, vegetables, and other crops. Although people spray pesticide when they see them, aphids are still there.

Let's rid ourselves of our hostility to these tiny creatures. Let's understand why they come. If we observe, we will discover that aphids normally live in grass, which is their home and source of food. When droughts come, they will breed fast and look for plants that contain juice, such as the buds of fruit trees or ears of corn. It is when the climate is abnormally dry that aphids become a disaster. In fact, reduction of some leaves during drought can decrease evaporation in trees, which is a kind of natural adjustment.

If we continue to observe, we will find that aphids disappear after it rains. When the drought goes away, new buds will grow. Aphids appearing on crops or fruit trees, suggests drought or lack of water. When we receive this message, we should take actions quickly to deal with the problem and care for the plants. Then aphids will disappear.

Insects are messengers of nature. However, it is not easy for arrogant human beings to understand the messages. Nature can't shout. When people refuse to understand, nature can just aggravate the problem until it draws our attention. If we can understand nature's messages and correct our behavior and the way we produce, we can make achievements more efficiently.[1]

Life on Her Work of Art

Zhang: What is life like on the farm? Every Monday we prepare the produce. Tuesday is a delivery day. On Wednesday we do more preparation and then deliver more on Thursday. On Friday we do whatever else we need to do.

We have three staff members. Two of them are a couple, the wife cooks and the husband delivers for me. We have a man from Yunnan now. He is a young China Agriculture University student here to work a semester with us. Villagers come out for the part-time work.

Several times I am the only one here. Especially in winter time. It was COLD this past year! I live here all year round.

We have several projects. See that construction there? (*pointing to a heap of lumber and tools*) We have been trying to build a washing room for many months, but there is not much progress because there is no time.

For the winter we store cabbage, carrots, etc. And we deliver in the winter because people need to eat then too. Each kind of produce has its own compost center and then there is a general compost in the southeastern part of the farm. This is very important but time intensive.

Listen to the birds, they are singing, they are happy. There are many kinds of birds here. We never catch them. There are also wild animals in my farm, rabbits, weasels, marmots, snakes etc.

This apple tree (crab apple) is not here just for its beauty. Its fruit is good for jam because it has such an interesting color. Cows like it. Cows like all kinds of fruits and they know where the fruits are. During the fruit season, we don't keep them in the pasture too much because they will eat all the fruit.

She takes one of the crab apples, and splits it with her knife. Then as we talk she fits the two pieces together and presses them together as we walk and talk.

We plant flowers for pest control. Some of them are also herbs and others help different kinds of ailments. They all attract insects and this way the insects won't attack the trees.

To be healthy you need to feel good in your body, psychologically, spiritually and connect with nature. Beauty can help you feel good. The local people who work for me think the flowers are just plants. Flowers are ways to take care of agriculture.

Come inside the workhouse. As you can see, it is also set up as a working area. This is where we do our organizing.

Points to a table and a pile of accounting books. The room is large, with tables and chairs.

We record our orders here and plan for the week. This afternoon, for instance, there will be a group of students, and they want me to tell them about organic agriculture. Later they will want to make dumplings.

Here, look at this crab apple fruit now. Now you see – the two sides were separated for quite a lot of time but the two are already sealing – the plant has life – but people don't realize and respect this. This is why I am here.

Stephanie: What is the role of the art of agriculture in Beijing's sustainable city of the future?

It is a very good question. Before talking about a sustainable city I'd like to talk how God's Grace Garden has practiced organic farming for 10 years. The restoration of nature is obvious. We have some new weeds, some new birds here. They enrich the diversity of my farm more and more every year.

Visitors asked me where I get the seeds for these weeds. But they grow themselves, they are not new to the earth, they've just come back. They are only new to us. I like weeds growing, even overgrowing in my farm. There isn't much land for them to grow freely today. I like weeds growing and I harvest them with gratitude, and so do my cows and lambs.

Birds hold concerts from time to time outside my window. They sing and dance with joy. I am their audience. I used to dream about the life of people in ancient times, but now it has become real again. It is not only in pictures, it is my true life. The birds won't just sing and dance here, they also hold big banquets here, they eat a lot of fruits and grain as they eat up the insects and weed seeds.

Some visitors suggested that I cover my fruit trees and my crops with some nets, but birds are not invaders. They are citizens. They enjoy their life here. The only problem is they have few places to go.

If there were more places like my farm, they could have more choice. People don't need to pay to look at birds in a zoo, where they can't sing and dance with joy. While birds choose to live in a biodynamic farm like God's

Grace Garden, many people choose to live in modern city, in artificial metal and concrete forests.

Today many people manage agriculture only for profit. The natural harmony is being lost. Agriculture should not be a business for farmers. Agriculture is human life. The aim of a business is profit, it is to make money. But life doesn't make money. Life may make profit, but the profit of life is happiness and the desire to continue to evolve and procreate for generations to come.

To build cities is human management. The larger the cities are, the bigger troubles they have. To build cities is a way to manage life. Urbanization means to consume. It is not the right way to enrich the lives of people. Urbanization is big business, a big stake of life. Urbanization is not life when it gives stress to the ecosystem. To be a sustainable city doesn't mean that the city enlarges itself, but that the human life there flourishes.

For life, the most important things are food, water, air and light. Food must be transported from far away. To keep the food "fresh," many additives are used so then the polluted food becomes just a kind of edible commodity.

Water is held in pipes in a confined limited cycle, unable to join the natural circling of the planet. In the artificial forests, the "light" is operated by the power of electricity. To operate cities, people need energy. Coal is being used up, and petroleum as well.

Maybe we'll find a new coal field to last another 30 years, but people who want to make money won't wait that long. They will develop the technology to finish that coalfield in 10 years. Maybe we can find huge coal deposits in the South Pole. Maybe we can estimate how much coal is there and how many years it can last, but they won't, they can't imagine, what life will be like after that.

Without energy, the monstrous city will become paralyzed. Before it is paralyzed, people will remember the land, the land that fed them for so long. But they will remember the land not to protect it but to use it to have the monster survive on bio-fuels. This will mean less food for people.

At least people recognize that crop fields are more sustainable than coal-fields. But with urbanization, land will become more and more limited. Now some refuse to encourage organic farming because they say organic farming cannot feed enough people. But how can we feed people if all the land is used to produce bio-fuel?

With limited and poor land quality, we have to decide whether to feed people first or to feed the city machine. Man evolved from the anthropoid ape, and what man will evolve into?

Plants that grow on the land only have roots. They can't walk. They are the food for animals who can walk. It is normal for animals to walk or run even, to seek their food. But cities ask people to grow plants with roots, and then ask the same people to carry that food to the residents in the city. Can this be sustainable?

People use some special plants to purify air. When people find that such plants really do help, they bring them into the city. Why can't they realize the value of the plants they eat? Why can't farms be accepted in the city? Why not appreciate the farmers who provide such wonderful nourishment?

Organic farms will be the stomach and lungs of the city. True organic farms supply safe food, purify the air, and enable living materials to be recycled. Organic farms will become the kitchen and garden for city residents.

We don't need to bring food from far away. We don't need to waste so much energy. We don't need to destroy nature to get resources, as mining does. Organic farms will be the link between farmers and urban residents. To have organic farms in the city is about creating a city where its residents foster their own art with nature. Through deepening respect for the soil, for all of nature around us, we city residents can create respect for the people who grow food that makes us healthy. Then the farmer will respond, just like nature will. Harmony through diversity. We all have a role to play.

Every week Zhang Zhimin sends members an order form. On it is her determination to help us all move forward to be part of our art project with nature:

尊重自然，与自然合作，自律地生活。

To respect Nature, to cooperate with Nature, to live with self-discipline.

有机农业，耕农田，耕心田。

Organic agriculture, land culture, mind culture.

一方水土养一方人，一方人养一方水土。

Land supports the people, the people support the land.

Yang Jing, Kites and Culture, Balancing the Traditional and the Fresh

I met Yang Jing (Jeff) out on the open fields near the Olympic Forest Park. Again I wanted to talk to someone unconnected to the field of sustainable development. Someone who enjoyed being outdoors. Someone who looked at the relationship between humans and nature from a personal perspective. I'd already decided that people who fly kites, and there are many in Beijing, might be the place to look. I reached out to some but was hesitant about taking too much of their time. They are really out to relax with their kites, after all. Old men who've been kiting for 20 years. Women coming out for the exercise. Some people like to kite together, but many like to sit quietly all day looking up at their connection to the sky.

Then I met Jeff. He was pulling on two strings and his kite was doing tricks. I wasn't sure he was the right person. He could speak German but not much English. I have no German and little Chinese. But when I asked him if he ever felt he had anything to say to the wind while kiting he said, yes, he did. He liked to talk to the wind. I knew I had my man.

Yang Jing posing where
I first met him

What I hadn't realized before we sat down for the interview was that Jeff was more than someone conscious of his relationship with nature. He was also going to show me what globalization can do for someone when you have the right spirit. When you make it work for you.

Globalization is both a positive and a negative today. It has created havoc, and made certain people rich and others much poorer. It is, however, a done deal. Now, we have to make it work for us. How can we make globalization today more valuable to us than it was yesterday?

Globalization has helped us transcend the limitations of our traditions. And while there used to be a concern about mass culture, the opposite has happened. Some cultures are even isolating themselves. But others are eager to use parts of what they learn from outside their borders and adapt it into their own future. Jeff seems to be such a person. Sport kiting brings him joy.

How we use our parks may become an important measure of a sustainable city in fact because people are part of the life of the city, the energy of the city. It is also where most of the city residents who are animals, birds and plants live too, of course.

Playing is connected to life. Life is connected to the soil. In Beijing's parks there are many people playing together or enjoying their solitude. For Chinese it is also about staying well despite the pressures of life.

"A sage prevents disease instead of treating disease and prevents chaos instead of suppressing chaos. To cure an illness after it has occurred, or to calm a disturbance after it was broken out is like digging a well when one already feels thirsty, or forging weapons after the war has taken place. Would these actions not be too late? The Yellow Emperor's Classic of Internal Medicine (Huangdi Neijing)."[1]

*****

Yang Jing: I was born in Beijing in '77 in Chongwenmen, which is in the south part of Beijing. I went to primary school, and then part of high school. Jinsong high school is a vocational school. It has a good reputation as a culinary school. Because I did well, I got to go to Germany in 1995 to study and work part time there. Other countries also give scholarships like the one I had, including the U.S. I worked my way through my final years of high school in Germany and learned to cook Western food, mostly German and French cuisine.

I became a chef and returned in 1997 at the age of 20. My first job was in a hotel in Beijing. Then a bar. Now I work at The Courtyard Gallery Restaurant, near Tiananmen Square. Clinton has been there.

I was just like my classmates but I guess more eager to learn about the world. I only had the most basic education. I knew little about foreign countries but I was really curious about them. Even before I went to Germany, I used to travel a lot to see the countryside of China.

Oh, when I was little, I played outside a lot. I especially liked the popular *shabao (cloth bags with sand inside)* like tag ball, and catch. And Chinese chess. I also loved, in the winter, to go out on the lakes and go "chair sledding" on the ice. We used the wooden sticks from ice cream bars to make small guns. We also played marbles. *(A look of delight as he remembers his favorites.)*

Sometimes I used newspapers and bamboo to make my own kite. There was no good string at that time.

I mainly played children's games, of course. Like beanbag games, and games like hopscotch and rubber band skip rope. We played cards, the colored-picture ones (flip one card to beat another card). We also rode little bikes. At that time there were not many bikes. I rode a bike with small wheels I borrowed from a friend.

Another game I liked was chess. I began to play chess in my third or fourth grade in primary school. I played with Western cards. But the games we play with these cards are different in China. The number of cards is also different.

Sometimes...I cannot figure out why, I found it very interesting to wander inside the Hutong *(the alleyways in the old parts of Beijing)* and try and find my way out. You never knew where you'd end up! I felt very good about this. It is a little like traveling.

I like to travel my way. I don't need to go see famous places. I like to travel naturally. When I see some beautiful place and it feels right, I will just get off the train. I may stay there for some time, even though there is nothing famous about it.

Stephanie: It is interesting that your cultural connection is with different kinds of games, not with food, not with festivals, but with anything that has to do with play.

Yang: I don't know where I got my skill at cooking. I didn't have a goal to be a fine chef. At the time, I didn't have a dream, or even a plan for my life. Both of my parents cooked Chinese food and I watched them but wasn't interested in it. To tell you the truth, I didn't like cooking much at first.

I am the kind of person who loves to be outside. I don't like to be inside. I just like to do things I enjoy.

I didn't really think much about my traditions or special festivals – ones other children look forward to. My connections were with my friends and what we did together. I come from an area of Beijing that is very old. We had more time than kids do today, so we were out a lot. We'd play all kinds of things – shuttlecock, top spinning, hoop rolling, or *kongzhu*. (*Kongzhu is a 2,000-year-old game like a double yoyo which spins and whistles*). Also sling shots. Some boys used to break other people's windows, but not me.

I think that a person needs to know more, learn new things, his whole life, instead of staying at home all the time, doing the same things over and over. If you stay at home, it is like being in a small world forever.

Playing is important to me. It makes me happy. I am not closed. I like to try different things, and it makes my life more colorful. Everyone says how time flies and we should put off our enjoyment until we have more money or time, or our condition improves. It may be too long in coming and arrive too late.

Yes, the job is very important. People must work hard to make money to have a secure life, but I don't want to be a miser. I will do my best to feel part of this wonderful world although I am not a rich man. Pleasure in life is most important, and I am enjoying life.

Germany

Yang: My cooking school was in Villengen, which is in the Black Forest area of Germany. The Black Forest is part of Baden-Wuerttemberg State. I studied during the week but on the weekends I'd travel around Europe.

It is more developed there. The quality of life is better. People are friendly and I felt comfortable. I learned German first by studying in Beijing for two years and then while I was there for the two years in Germany along with my other studies. This was a thorough program that the Germans set up and they prepared me very well for my career.

Very few people flew the kites there. Some children rode bikes in the parks, with helmets. Some children played with rollerblades. Some older people took walks in the parks. I saw very few young people there. The young people prefer to go to the plazas and play some...how to say it...some extreme sports, such as the BMX (Bicycle Motocross) that can spin and such.

I found that German people really make sure to protect themselves with helmets and such. Not like us. We rarely use such protection, except for those who are professionals. German people will not allow themselves to get hurt. They feel strongly about this.

Stephanie: Before, in the U.S there were many games like hoops and marbles. But now we are more like Germany. We want the best and newest thing – whatever is coolest. Where did that come from I wonder?

Yang: But I think that it is not the same in China. The young people elsewhere play different games than we do. For example, it is very common for us to go to the parks or play outside. But if you said "Let's play or take a walk in the park," in other countries, it would be an unusual thing to hear.

They prefer to have a cup of coffee in a coffee shop, or to go to the disco, or to travel or something. These activities are more common for them.

They don't often go to parks, to play outside. Except for team sports, of course.

These kids looked very professional but they were probably beginners. All of them dressed the part of being a biker, or a rollerblader, and such. And always well equipped.

Kiting Today

Yang: In fact sport kiting is very different from the one-string kite. After you fly the one-string kite into the sky, you can do nothing more with it. What you focus on more is the process of making a kite. That is where the fun is. But after you fly it, you leave it alone and do nothing. But the two-string kite is a sports kite.

The sport kite has a triangular delta shape and is controlled by two strings. These kites are normally constructed from lightweight plastic with spars. The flying lines are made so that they are light, don't stretch and stay slippery even when wrapped many times.

You can walk, run forward or backwards and give the lines different amounts of tension. By pulling and pushing, you can do complex tricks and patterns, turning, looping, landings, flipping, and floating maneuvers are normal parts of the sport. During diving maneuvers sport kites can reach high speeds, and then stall and be motionless. Acrobatics and dancing to music are also part of the enjoyment.[2]

Yang: I started when I got back to Beijing. I hadn't heard about it in Europe. One day I went to Chaoyang Park and came across several people doing it. They were amongst the first to know about it in China. They were Chinese. I'd only seen it on TV. They played very well and I really wanted to learn.

When you begin, you can only make the kite fly in a circle. Most people can do this after practicing three or four times. There are two strings that control the kite. You pull the string to the left to make it fly to the left, and pull the string to the right to make it go right.

The kites can make sounds. Most sport kites can make sounds like a war plane. Many people love this. It makes them feel cool. A sport kite has a strong force that pulls you along with its power. So you have the feeling that you are really controlling something wild. You have a strong feeling of achievement, like driving a car. So this is the most fascinating part at the beginning.

There is a difference between amateurs and professionals. There are standards to judge whether a person is "good" and "not good enough." If you fly the kite in a circle, it must be a circle, not (*demonstrates*) an egg! This is the standard of "good." This is the simplest. Some people can make the kite create a triangle, but good ones must make an equilateral triangle.

You also must control the speed of the kite. There must be a change of speed; otherwise, there is no impact for audiences. Everything is controlled by skill. People judge to what degree the players can meet the standard. There are international standards and rules.

There are many contests in the United States. There are contests in Beijing too. But I don't go. I am not interested. Because...you know there are certain characteristics to such events, such as "If I want you to get first price, you can win." (*Ha, ha, ha.*) So I do not care for such contests. I just like playing. I don't care whether I win a prize or not.

Stephanie: You mean that in the contests, for example, if there are two people who fly the kites in a circle, the judge can decide which one is the winner?

Yang: It cannot be so obvious. (*laughs*)

Yang: There are speed contests too. The wind must be very strong, of course. Without wind, there is no speed. People can fly the kite at a level five or six wind velocity, if you and your kite can bear the wind. 150 km/hour is the average. There is equipment to measure the speed. You draw a line on the ground and put a gadget there. When the kite flies over the line, it measures the speed. There are some very famous contests in France.

It is also possible to fly five kites at the same time. Since there are two strings, you can use both your hands to control the kite. But you can use one hand to control the strings if they are on a handle with two rings on the left and right. You can use one hand to control two strings. What if there are three strings on the handle? And what if there is a handle with two strings on your knee? So you already have five kites on your body. (*He grins with delight.*)

In general anybody can fly three kites at the same time. If you want to play five kites at the same time, again the wind must be strong enough. Otherwise, the kites cannot fly up. So more people fly kites with both hands. If you want, you can add a kite at your waist, but it is more difficult.

There is also a four-string kite. It has a string for acceleration, another string for the brake. If you pull the accelerator, it is like in a car, the kite will face upward against the wind and it goes up. If you pull the string for the brake, it faces down so it stops. So this kind of kite can fly, stop, and go around, fly and stop... We can also create shapes. The kite is called a "quad-line."

The length of the string does not change when you fly it. However, there are different lengths for the kite. You can fly it with 5-meter strings, 10-meter strings, 15-meters, 20-meters, 33-meters, and over 50-meter strings. The lengths of the strings are different, so their expressive force is different. But there is no rolling up or out of the string.

There are many shapes the kites can make while moving. They are all have standards. There is no requirement for what kind of kite you use. You can buy it or make it. They only require that you meet the standard, that you create the standard kite.

This sport's history is very short – only 20 years. So there are not many people doing it.

Stephanie: China is supposed to have invented the kite. Do you know much about the history of kiting? Can you describe some of the kinds of kites?

Yang: It was long, long time ago. At that time the kite was called "Yuan made of paper"(纸鸢) (*Yuan is a kind of bird.*) There are several theories about the history and not everyone agrees. Now the kite is called "Fengzheng"(风筝).

There is no clear history, like the much shorter history of sport kites. The sport kite is definitely from abroad. There are no different opinions. But as for the one-string traditional kiting, there are different opinions about its history. I don't know too much about the one-string traditional kite. It seems there were kites in the Song Dynasty (960-1279), but I think the earliest records of kites was in the Zhou Dynasty (1045-256 BCE). In the Song Dynasty there was the belief that when your kite was high in the sky and you cut the string, then all of your bad fortune would go up with the kite.

There is a kind of one-string kite in Beijing, which is called *shayan* (沙燕). Once they get them in the sky, people don't pull them down either. People fly such kites during festivals, because they want their bad luck to fly away. So they cut the string of the kite. They want life to be better. This is a very traditional thing in Beijing.

I like the traditional shayan in Beijing. There are different types of shayan. Some are fat, some are thin. They are all different.

Tibet has kites on which they paint sacred signs. The square shape of the kite means that this is a fighting kite. Tibetans grind glass then mix it with rice paste, then coat the string with this special rice glue. When the kites go up, they try to cut the string of the competing kite. Since they have flat-roof houses, when they fly the kites, all the people in the village stand on the flat roofs and watch.

This kind of kiting is also popular in India and many countries in the South-east. There are contests there too – testing the skill of cutting the string, secret recipes for the glass glue and special silk for the strings and so on. There are countries that forbid this kind of kiting as well. It can be danger-ous.

The fighting kite is called *Doujianzi* (斗尖子) in China. There are people who play here, but it is not so popular. The fighting kite is a kind of one-string kite. It requires technical skill. People want to cut the string quickly so they can win.

There are also many ways to fight. One way is to pull on the string. Or put the string on the ground, pull and fight. Another way is to use a bit of cloth, like denim. Rub the kite's strings against each other's cloth, to see who can rub it faster and more strongly so the other string breaks. This is more difficult. There are contests like this in Weifang, Shandong Province.

There are other uses for kites. They were used in ancient times for military purposes. More recently for example, some have put a camera on a kite to take pictures from up above. It is also used for fishing. People attach a hook to a kite above a lake. They let the kite out low over the lake and wait for the fish. But this is not serious. It is just for fun.

There is *penger* (碰儿). This is a "butterfly" kite with two wings and a knot on the string. The kite can climb up along the string. The two wings that which are against the wind can fly up and hit a rubber line on the kite, which makes the two wings close so the kite falls. So it can go up and down, up and down... So it is very interesting. Many people play with these.

There are night-flying kite enthusiasts as well. All lit up like fireworks. Sometimes 15-20 kites on a string. Beautiful.

My Sport Kite Hobby

Yang: Once I learned how to fly, I made a website www.balletkite.com.

My friends that I play with now, found me through my website. We play once a week on Saturdays from 1 p.m. From 5 to 20 people come depending on the day. Beginners continue to contact me through the website. Sometimes we eat together afterwards. We have groups as well in Dalian, Qinghuangdao and Guangzhou. They are by the ocean so the wind is very good.

We don't perform often. We just come to practice – about four hours. We have become friends. There is no leader, we just play together. It is very relaxed. We play up north of the Olympic Park area. Where you found me.

When we were in our 20s, we'd stay all day long, bring food and eat together. Most of us are men. Some children about seven years old and some women. Our oldest player is in his 60s. My wife and daughter also come.

Ballet kiting is kiting with music. You fly the kite to music. I think this is the top level of playing. American people know a lot more about this. We learned and developed our own skill using foreign websites, by discussing how to perform what we saw.

We mainly practice techniques and develop our skills. There are many kinds of ballet kiting. One is the two-string kite, and another is the three-string kite and more-string kite.

You can use any kind of music. When the wind is soft, you can use some soft music. Otherwise you cannot give the right impression. There is individual ballet and double ballet. There are also ballets performed by a team. I remember the world record is a team of 56 people.

The wind matters in sport kiting. The wind, the music, your heart and your

Yang Jing doing six at
a time at the beach

[Yang Jing, Kites and Culture, Balancing the Traditional and the Fresh]

relationship with nature – there is nothing like it! Your whole body is connected and in rhythm with what you are orchestrating with your arms. You are like the conductor with two batons!

When you do a duet, your synchronization with your partner adds another dimension. You have to practice be in sync. Precise in the movement of your fingers. More like a musical duet between two people yet different since you are not in eye contact. You have to feel the sync on the ground and then look up into the sky to see the result. It too is wonderful and a test of your skill.

The kite is a certain distance, and so the skill is how you use your fingers and joints to play. This is where the skill lies. You are playing a silent instrument by communicating with your body. The more sensitive you are, the more beautifully you will "play" your "instrument."

This kind of kiting gives you a good workout for your joints and fingers. It is also good for your neck. Everyone knows that kiting is good for your health.

Stephanie: What is it about the neck that is so important? When I asked other kiters why they kite, they immediately touched the back of their necks and looked at me meaningfully.

Yang: This is a big problem today. People sit and look down all day long. At the computer, table or desk. Many kinds of problems occur because of this, blood pressure problems, heart problems and so on.

This is a Chinese way of thinking, but actually it makes sense. If you have a problem in your neck, you can have a problem in the brain, heart and elsewhere. It is also known to be connected to apoplexy, stroke and palsy. So exercising your neck muscles can help.

Then there is the small motor control exercise when you combine the action of your eye, hand, brain and fingers. You won't understand this if you only think linearly.

Stephanie: Another example of how traditional wisdom and the modern world can coexist and enrich one another.

Yang: I love flying kites. You know, people living in big cities have a lot of pressure. When I see my kite up in the sky there – the kite and the blue sky – my problems go away. It makes me relax and happy.

You need to deepen your skills, and you need practice. I immerse myself in such trick-flying, and the tricks become more and more complex so I need to develop my skill. You can create and invent new tricks and create your own routines. I like the novelty and creativeness. If you fly well, you can fly surrounded by music and dance. You can show sadness, happiness, anger and so on. A kite has vitality just like you. If you communicate with the kite and the wind and talk with this nature, you can really feel its pure life. You can keep a cool and calm mind, care about others and be optimistic.

Sustainable City and Nature

Yang: Development should not be about how modern a place is but rather how healthy the common people are. Developing the skills of kiting is real development. Good play is also a way to develop the city into a sustainable one.

Now there are fewer people in the parks than before. There are too many buildings so space is limited. Maybe the city got developed, but people can't be as healthy.

I believe when I am kiting, I am part of nature again. I like to relax and be together with nature. I also to camp and hike. I feel very good when I get to the top of a mountain with the great sky above me and mountains all around. It is like my experience with kiting. It releases pressure and makes you stronger so you can face difficulties.

I was mad about mountain climbing and camping for a period of time. Mountain climbing also lets you feel that you have accomplished something. You have surpassed yourself. It is also a kind of test of your ability to endure. And then when you come across difficulties in your own life, you find you are no longer so weak.

[Yang Jing, Kites and Culture, Balancing the Traditional and the Fresh]

Stephanie: Mao Zedong once said that nature is there to test us.

Yang: Yes, yes. And you create good friends through hiking together. Some people who are under great pressure and whose nerves are very tight, when they see nature, they burst into tears to witness such beauty. Because nature is very profound and strong. When people are in nature, this kind of thing happens.

It is a kind of pure feeling because there is no economic interest. People feel that they want to help one another. You are totally relaxed and you feel the vastness of your mind. There is no pressure.

Especially nowadays, the relationships between people are very subtle. But the nature is not like that. So we need nature in our lives. Everyone needs to have access to nature, to test ourselves, to step outside our normal lives.

Nature makes you feel pure and simple. More real. The bonding you experience sharing an adventure together is hard to find in normal life. Relationships are more natural. More pure and simple too. And we help each other. That is to say...how to say it...a kind of "standing together regardless of the situation."

In fact when we went to Little Wutai Mountain there was an incident. When we were at the altitude of 2,800 meters, it began to rain. We were halfway up the mountain and we couldn't decide to climb up or go down. There were more than 10 people in our group.

We couldn't move because of the abyss next to the path where we stood in the rain. The path became very slippery. We could die if we fell. So the men and the women helped each other and created a shelter to wait out the weather. We formed very good relationships. That feeling, like the feeling – that we will live and die side by side—this is one of the reasons why I like hiking.

Kiting has some things in common with hiking. You can regard them as toys or you can also regard them as friends that play with you. If you devote your energy and time to them, they can also express some emotions like a human being. My kite is like this. It is creative.

What I mean by "creative" is that once I mastered the many basic move-ments, I connected with the kite in so many ways. Sharing a time in my own private dance. It is like building blocks. Everybody builds different things. So I say there is a lot of creativity. This is what attracts people.

I always think that if you communicate with the kite, it will have feelings too. We can say it this way, although it is only a "thing" of plastic and sticks.

You can treat your kite like a toy or like a partner. If you fuse with the kite, it will reflect your feeling. If you deeply connect the kite – the kite will respond.

We can choose how we want to do it but we all need nature in our lives. A sustainable city means one where the residents build deep relationships with nature. This kind of energy will ensure long-term sustainability, because life in the city and nature are in accord.

Globalization and Yang Jing

Yang: We live in apartments and many of us don't know the names of our neighbors. I prefer the old way when people lived in harmony. But there is no way to stop development, and I play with kites that express the tradi-tional and the new at the same time.

Not many people do sport kiting. It is kind of expensive – $400-$500. Then there is a language problem. Some of us can only look at the website but can't read anything. There is no dialogue between them and players else-where. I try and help them. For myself, traveling helped me see the wider world.

But even though many people travel, some come back the same. My Chinese classmates in Germany were lazy. They thought they were okay the way they were and didn't get to know the culture there. They came home unable to speak German. I was different. I wanted to know. Like with the kites – I took the initiative to talk with people and set up my hobby. I guess I am open-minded. I like to talk with foreigners and get new ideas. You and me. Open-hearted people have initiative.

I think about traditional and modern culture. The traditional culture can be preserved. But...how to say it.... The modern ones are not that substantial. What has history is more profound.

I feel that skyscrapers are not as harmonious as the traditional courtyard houses. Before, in the courtyard houses, the relationships between people were more interactive. But when people move into skyscrapers, they tear up their roots and make their home in a new place. They can't depend on neighbors. They don't even know them.

We are more and more modernized, but the relationships between people have grown weaker and weaker. Maybe modern means more profits, but I prefer traditional life.

The restaurant I work for is in a courtyard house and there are many of them around it. Many of our clientele come from tourist agencies. Some expats come back a lot because they know us.

I think that we should not resist all modern things though. Although I like traditional things, I connect with the modern every day. We can connect though on our own terms. The kite I play with, for example. There wasn't any information about them in China. So I browsed around foreign web-sites, and learned and absorbed their advanced moves. This is how I create the balance that is right for me.

Stephanie: And you are particularly good at globalization. So what's your secret?

Yang: Secret? (*laughs*) I feel that...how to say it...in fact I treasure the traditional, but I must absorb new things in order to develop, right? Take the sport kite, for example, I want to always get better. Polish my skills.

I want to try my best to keep myself at the international standard in this field. But we are very isolated here and it is like working behind closed doors. We are trying now to add some Chinese features, just for ourselves. But we also need to see what others are doing so we can better ourselves.

I understand some English and I have connected with foreign players and websites. At least I can discuss questions online. I can do this. But other Chinese players can't. What they do is just to open the website to see whether there is a new video. Very few communicate with foreign players. So I feel that we are very insular at this stage and that is why we have developed slowly.

If you are very old fashioned and traditional, you will know only what can be seen and experienced here in Beijing. On the other hand, bad modern is bad modern. A city that doesn't help its residents become healthier is modern but not right.

Because I can communicate in German, I can participate on German online forums about kiting and bring in new ideas for my group. It is the newness – modern in the right way, I suppose. That is what we need to recognize and to value.

It is so much more fun to be very friendly. When we get close with each other, we can learn a lot. We learn the strengths of others and polish ourselves. Germans are also traditional and modern too. We are creating the new – just by talking together. So we both grow.

Betsy Damon, Visionary for a Living Water Sustainable Future

My sister-in-law, Jean Tansey, an artist and a member of Betsy's No Limits for Women Artists, introduced me to Betsy Damon in Beijing in 1995. Betsy Damon is the director of Keepers of the Waters. Keepers is a U.S.-based non-profit organization that serves as an international communications network for people actively engaged in projects that transform our relationship with water.

Betsy Damon in Beijing

At the time she was working on a project in Chengdu called the Living Water Garden. Betsy, an internationally known performance and installation artist since 1985, has focused her practice on water. She has devoted her life to creating awareness of the life inside water. Through her art she demonstrates how live water is essential to life. She has safeguarded springs, taught city bureaucrats how to manage and restore their water systems, initiated community actions to remediate local water sources, all because of her deep conviction that we need healthy water to live wisely enough to create a future for humankind.

She once explained to me what healthy water means. In the Netherlands they tested two kinds of water systems. Dirty water was sent two ways – one way was down a flow-form system of vortices and the other down a system of flat cement steps – both ending in pools. Although the dissolved oxygen was the same in both systems, at the end the water from the step system contained no life forms and no plants grew. In the other system, flowering plants grew upon which thrived insects and butterflies. Water that is able to move in a vortex motion is primary to a biodynamic environment.

Whether visibly or invisibly, water always moves in vortices. Water quality deteriorates when it moves through a straight-lined system, such as in piping. It is the movement of water which is the genesis of form. All forms are the movement of water stopped.

She explained that water that moves in created vortices, enables oxygen and hydrogen to move with greater flexibility. If you look at waterfalls and various flowing systems, like rivers, this is what it wants to do naturally. Look at rocks, trees, leaves, bones, and hearts. Movement is the motion of life, or form-becoming. We can not separate out water from form. It is form, and in living water you can see clearly that it has form. It creates vortexes and layers of waves, which when they cross do not interrupt each other. You can see much, much more if you look through a microscope.

The Living Water Garden (1998) is a six-acre park that revives water from a polluted river through a seven-stage cleaning system. It includes a settling pond, aeration system, constructed wetlands, and filtering ponds to clean water to contact quality. The park contains an environmental education center with sculptural/educational elements throughout. Included are water forms that encourage the water to move in a vortices system. Once cleaned, the water goes out into the park area and back into the river.

In 1998, the former Prime Minister, Zhu Rongji, who initially opposed the park, later declared it the best model of environmental education in the country.

Living Water Garden

[Betsy Damon, Visionary for a Living Water Sustainable Future]

It is included on tourist maps, visited by most mayors of China, and has spread eco-solutions throughout China and much of the world. The principles behind the Living Water Garden are taught as examples of innovative solutions to urban water run-off. It has opened the door for a dialogue to challenge the normal policy of development in which engineering solves all problems. Millions of people have been exposed to this solution via many media outlets such as the BBC radio, and newspaper and magazines in China and the U.S.

After this success, the Beijing Bureau of Hydraulic Engineering, Research and Design invited Betsy to the capital to teach ecological river design and restoration. She has also been a consultant for projects in cities throughout in the U.S.A., including Duluth, Minnesota; Portland, Oregon; St Louis, Missouri; and Dallas, Texas. In China she has worked in Nanning and Baihei, Guanxi, Zhuang Autonomous Region and Hong Zhou and Shenzhen, in Guangdong Province.

In 2002 she helped establish the Chengdu Urban River Association (CURA) in Sichuan, China, and continues to serve as a consultant to CURA. Its mission is to restore and preserve the rivers in the watershed of Chengdu. She provides training sessions, lectures, mentors interns and raises funds. Right now CURA is focused on reusing solid waste. For 3,000 years solid waste was the basis for sustainable farming in China. CURA is now promoting separation toilets in rural areas as an advanced and convenient way to restore the soil and the water.

Betsy and I reunited in a hotel on the west side of the city. I saw her briefly last year for an evening, but before that it had been years since we'd seen each other – and lo and behold, it was to be in Beijing again.

*****

Environmental Artist

"Water is the foundation of life, the connective tissue of the universe. Therefore, sustaining the water systems must be the foundation of planning and development." – Betsy Damon

Betsy Damon: Our mission at Keepers of the Waters is to inspire and promote projects that restore, preserve and remediate water sources using a combination of art, science, and community involvement. Science is the base of information from which people need to understand the issue; art is the means of communication and inspiration; community involvement brings in all those who wish to restore and preserve water quality. Blending these disciplines helps make the natural process of water treatment both visible and integrated into our daily life and social culture.

Global water quality is dependent on each community having a sustainable water source that they know about and feel responsible for. Cities all over the planet can be filled with vibrant community centers, parks, schoolyards, businesses and backyards filled with living water and art. These will help people become and stay intimately connected to their water sources. These projects will lead the way for fully sustainable water infrastructures, visible and integrated into our daily lives, rather than hidden under the ground.

When people join together to solve a problem, they do it better than when they do it alone. Through water, we interconnect and relate to all other living things. Like water, we are one giant family, always seeking to join one another.

Betsy Damon and the Spirit of Art

Stephanie: You've worked with a lot of Chinese artists. Are they like you? Do they understand how important water is?

Betsy: I have worked with many Chinese artists. We are not all made to walk on this world in the same way. So I hesitate to say you should do this or that. The best I think I can do is open a door, and when I open a door, the people who are ready, step through it. So I am not alone or struggling all of the time. Like with Latso, the Tibetan woman who is now my collaborator. It took three conversations before I trusted her with $5,000 to go back to Tibet and film the uplands. Trusted her and gave it to her. No contract no nothing.

Water Is Life

Betsy: People don't understand what water quality really means for the development of life. Most people think water is just water. Now, fortunately cell biologists have actually begun to study the water in our cells, not just the protein.

They are discovering that the water in our cells is actually an H_2O gel that is not found anywhere else. DNA, the double helix, is the longest living biological form that we now know of and it is sheathed in a fine film of water. The movement of the protein is made possible by the water connections. Here you see that water is integrated at the most basic building block of our lives. I see this as an indicator that our health and livelihood are intimately connected with the health of water. Our DNA only works because of water.

Scientists have actually noticed that only 2% of your body is protein and water is everything else. They have found that there is a special gel – it is an H_2O gel – that is in your cells – and not anywhere else.

Listen, this is so exciting! They've been able to see what happens at conception. At the very beginning, the baby is a perfectly bilateral form. It has a mind and it is exactly symmetrical. There is a tiny mind but there is no heart yet. There is a kind of gel of water surrounding this mind. And that water sheathed over the brain then moves in vortices and creates the heart. This is at around two weeks.

Knowing this, I assume that water quality, that is, water with dissolved minerals that vibrates with life, is what human beings need. Not distilled water, not water that has chlorine, ammonia or fluoride.

I was so blown away.

Stephanie: You are kidding me!

No. Water is the heart-mind connection. So the vortex is how water moves. The vortex is the primary recreating form of our universe. What are we doing to it when we dam, pollute and straighten our rivers? We are disconnecting the very heartbeat of the earth.

So if we are not drinking good water, if we drink plastic water, or sodas, of course, we are going to get sick. Of course, we are going to get cancers. Suddenly your whole system collapses because the water in your body has chemicals in it. We identify cancers as coming from various parts of our bodies. Or it just might be that because we drink polluted water and our bodies are mostly water, we are going to sicken somewhere. What are we doing?! My real passion is to connect people to being alive. You have to have quality water to be alive. There is no substitute for this at all.

Betsy Supports Beijing Rivers

When I was here from (2000-2006). I diagrammed for the Hydraulic Engineering and Research Bureau how to do planning and design. Other priorities bogged many of our plans down. We worked with the planning bureau to create integrated planning, which meant integrating effluent from waste water treatment plants and capturing storm water run off and wherever possible, restoring or preserving a river's contact with earth, as well as implementing wetlands.

The Beijing Bureau invited me to create an ecological design team for the Tongzhou District, a suburb of Beijing. This was the part of the city that was the end of the Grand Canal, which went from Hangzhou and Shanghai to Beijing. Tongzhou is a town that was absorbed into the municipality. Its population is less than 1 million with a planned population of more than 4 million, and its water supply is already too little per capita. In our plan, all the storm water and gray water in the design areas were recycled and cleaned through biological systems, which included solar aquatics, and wetland and aeration systems.

In 2004 we won an award for a design and management concept for a sustainable system for the Wenyu River in Beijing. The design team included both foreign and Chinese companies. The design area was 45 sq. km with 23 km on the river itself. Water is in great shortage in the Beijing area. Therefore, all water used was recycled through numerous systems from solar aquatics to agricultural production and even re-infiltration of forests.

In Beijing rivers are divided between districts, and we were designing the western side. It was a huge competition and the one we did was totally based on what the U.N. has recommended – how much heavily populated space and how much wild space you have to have, to keep our planet sustainable. You need to keep 66% wild and 40% of that absolutely wild. We came up with a design for the western side that reused every single drop of water that came in, to create productive forests or orchards and concentrated the people so rainwater could be collected.

The result was the Wenyu River is not hardscape. That is the best I can say. They didn't put concrete on its edges so this allows the water and the land to connect – a vital interaction. They also reduced the number of golf courses around it. Perhaps also the plan ended up protecting green spaces on the river on the one side. I also helped the Bureau design an ecological master plan for the entire Wenyu River system.

The Yongding River on the western side of Beijing is being revitalized. The claim is that it is a sustainable design. The water table has been so depleted that even if there is a large rainfall you never see any water, because the ground is a sandy and permeable surface. So, to create an illusion of water, first they lined the riverbed with plastic, and then piped effluent water from wastewater treatment plants 50 kilometers away. They have created vast wetlands to treat the effluent, and utilized the natural gradient to allow for aeration. They have maintained the original width of the river.

Two design experts and I did a daylong workshop with the design team from the Hydraulic Bureau. Ideally, the water, that would create an illusion of a river, should be water that is sourced from the area. They are creating a development out there for several million people. So, the new development will need to provide the water. Additionally, this riverbed needs to be much more narrower and deeper, if they want to create a more viable, dynamic ecosystem.

I will say that they tried very hard, but the reality is that the planning and development to integrate all systems involved are still too limited.

I also created a design team for the Olympic Forest Park project in collaboration with Turin, a landscape company. We were chosen by the Olympic Committee and the Beijing Bureau to be one of eight to enter an international competition. Our design is now the foundation of the park's sustainable water system. This was the only design submitted that included a comprehensive sustainable solution for the Olympic Park.

Margo Young of EDM Canada and I were responsible for the concept plan for the water system. In order to have a comprehensive water plan, we had to understand what the water sources are, what the water quality is as well as the natural topography that we were dealing with. We sought to have an interconnected water system that would maintain the water quality for the entire site. The part of our system that was integrated into the final design was the vast protected wetlands.

This park, as part of the 2008 Olympics, could become the model for sustainable cities. It is a 21st century solution for water management. It will clean the water to a level suitable for significant human contact.

Along the way, I wrote sustainable and ecological guidelines for the Beijing Urban Planning Bureau, diagramming for them how to create cross-departmental collaborations for ecological planning. Many of the principles I taught here in Beijing are still used. But what they need to do is to make sure there is rainwater harvesting. So they can live off their own rain and water use. Beijing sources its water from far away now.

My time in Beijing was about education. I walked along every river in Beijing with the people from the Planning Bureau. I showed them why they need to respect the edge where the water meets the earth. This is what starts a microsystem. These microsystems are totally important to the world even if it is only for this river. Where water meets earth is where everything happens. Where life is born. Where plants come from. Where insects live. If you go in and bulldoze it every year, you are systematically forcing life to recreate itself over and over again instead of developing into more complex life.

Beijing is a myth, in the sense that it has no sustainable base. It has depleted its water sources. Beijing has taken all of the water from the mountains. That is why the hills are so dry and the plants can't grow. They are planting many trees on the lowlands, but that is no solution.

Beijing's Water Problems – Background

Today Beijing has severe water problems. Its two reservoirs hold 100 cubic meters per person, far below the international warning level. At the same time population has swelled to over 19 million.

Unfortunately, the municipality faces an impossible reality: It cannot easily curb the rising population which continues to be such an incredible strain on the ecosystem. This current government is not the first to have water problems on this very spot. Nor the first to look for engineering solutions.

During the Yuan Dynasty (1271- 1368) there were already water problems. The Grand Canal was completed to help supply the city with water. During the Ming Dynasty (1368-1644), moats were constructed around the Forbidden City – now this is some of Second Ring Road. These moats performed the multiple functions of water supply, sewage treatment, transportation and defense. The lakes north and northwest of the Forbidden City were part of this plan.

During the Qing Dynasty (1636-1911) the Yongding River flooded every four years during its 268-year rule. Several times the capital was completely flooded. What is now the western part of Beijing was filled with fish, waterfowl, lotus and paddy fields, and all irrigated by the river.

The Yongding River, because of its heavy silt and turbulent torrents during the high water season, was first known as Wuding River, meaning "capricious river." People wished it to be permanently stable, so it was renamed the Yongding River (meaning "settled forever" in Chinese). It has been dry for more than a decade, and the water released into it comes from an effluent reservoir upstream.

Today desertification encroaching on the city, overuse of rivers and perhaps to a large extent, rapid urbanization are some of the reasons why Beijing water problems are so severe. Today, there is the South North Water Transfer Project, a monumental and controversial undertaking to bring the water of the Yangtze River up to Beijing. The first of the water transfer system has already reached Beijing and the second plan will be complete in 2014.

Sources of Water

Beijing sits on the alluvial plain between the Yongding River and the Chaobai River. The Yongding River runs down from the Taihang Mountains from the Northeast. The Chaobai River runs from Yanshan Mountains in the west and flows to the east of Beijing. In the past few decades, some large dams have been built on the river to form the Miyun and Huairou reservoirs. These provide the water for Beijing's canals and lakes as well as drinking water.

The Grand Canal of China

The Grand Canal of China, the longest man-made waterway in the world, and the earliest, begins in Hangzhou in East China (south from Beijing) and terminates in Beijing, running for a total length of 1,794 kilometers. Digging started in the late Spring and Autumn Period (about the 5th century BCE), and it was twice extended and widened, during the Sui (581-618) and Yuan dynasties.

The Grand Canal comes in via Tianjin to the south. From Tianjin it heads northwest, for a short time following the course of the Yongding River. The canal then branches off towards Tongzhou. A Grand Canal Cultural Park has been built.

The final extension of the canal connects Tongzhou with a wharf called the Houhai or 'rear sea' in central Beijing. In the Ming and Qing dynasties, however, the water level in the Tonghui River dropped and it was impossible for ships to travel from Tongzhou to Beijing. Tongzhou again became the northern shipping terminus of the canal. Cargoes were unloaded at Tongzhou and transported to Beijing by land, which cost as much in transportation costs as the entire northern trip to Tongzhou. The Tonghui River still

Betsy in contact with living water

exists as a wide, concrete lined storm channel and drain for the suburbs of Beijing.

Because China's terrain slopes eastward – from the highlands and mountains in the west to the hinterlands on the shore of the Pacific – all the major rivers in China run west to east. The Grand Canal is the sole waterway for south-north transportation and communication. It enabled Beijing in the past to become a prosperous trading center. Highways and railways have gradually replaced the Grand Canal as a means of transportation.

Beijing's Lakes and Wells

Most of the lakes in Beijing are manmade. However Lotus Lake near the Beijing West Railroad Station was natural in the past and used by the Ji and Yan peoples as a reservoir. It is now also encased in plastic.

One of the busiest shopping districts in Beijing today is Wangfujing, which means, "Well of the Prince's Mansion." Wangfujing owes its name to the fine quality of the water from two wells on two side streets. In the past, Beijing *residents relied on water drawn from such wells. Unfortunately, most of the wells produced salty or bitter water. Fine quality well water was sold at a good price. The imperial family only drank water from the springs in the Western Hills.*

Stephanie: So what are you doing now?

Betsy: Realizing what was happening in Beijing with its water problems, and knowing what happened in Los Angeles, I began to look at uplands where rivers begin. There are micro solutions and macro solutions that can be studied and implemented to help resolve urban problems.

In early 1992, I learned that in the mountains surrounding Chengdu, there was a living water culture, primarily of Tibetans. In 2007 I found another extensive water culture in western Sichuan. Then in 2008 I stumbled into a Tibetan store at 9 p.m. in New York and was invited to drink barley tea. This is how I met my present collaborator. Two evenings later, we became partners.

In 2009 we traveled together to these locations for a month. Everyone knew her, every village leader, every head of a monastery. We initiated a cleanup at a monastery where the river was a dumping ground for plastics. Two years later in 2011, when we visited again, we saw they really have kept the place clean.

The villages are losing their water because of the damming. So we've begun to discuss with them how to implement integrated wastewater/energy solutions using with rainwater harvesting. We created relationships for the future. We are continuing to do research there.

I am trying to raise money for a wastewater treatment system for 100 people. Completely natural and recycled. I want to help them put in microsolutions.

In Sichuan we went to this one site, very mountainous. At this spring in the rocks, we found a character painting on one of the boulders. "It is declared that this mountain cannot be disturbed. Nobody can cut trees down and don't let your cattle feed here – because this water source is sacred." This was 300 years ago.

Everywhere I go, I discover places like this. Where people understand the fragile conditions of water. Then mining and damming has come in. Like, wow it's beautiful, let's mess with it! Make progress!

I cried really hard after my trip to Sichuan. I can't imagine traveling around the United States and being so welcomed at the last minute into a poor farmhouse. Even as I thought, "Uhhh, I don't really want to stay here." *(laughs)*

And I was carried across a river, a raging river, on the back of a big farmer last week, because I definitely could not walk on the tree trunks. I couldn't. And it wasn't possible to go on your butt because there were still branches sticking out.

Everywhere we went, people were so happy to tell us about their waters. They were so proud of them, yet they were distressed by the depletion caused by development, industry and extraction. They still live very close to the land. They are connected. They know which waters are really good for health.

It is very confusing when electricity comes in because of a dam. There is an expectation of things becoming better. But often citizens rapidly discover that they have lost the means to take care of themselves.

The old people – their focus is to be healthy – because there won't be anyone else to fix them. A hundred years ago people were at least strong. Their life and labor made them this way. Now we have to learn to do this again – to live in the same place over and over again – just like the Chinese did for so long.

Aba County in Sichuan has banned plastics. They actually banned them. These people are one step away from being herders, so they know the grasslands. They know farming and if real respect for this knowledge can be the basis for doing what needs to be implemented, then it is not a big job to help them be sustainable for the foreseeable future.

Even people who come in, with visions of hotels and resorts, to help alleviate their poverty, or to write protective policies for them, wind up not really helping in the long run. People have to stand up and create the right policies for themselves.

Uplands Adaptation to Climate Change

We also need macro projects. Since I have been working at the 8,000 to 12,000 foot altitude with the Tibetan culture, I have been invited into an upland adaptation project for climate change initiated by Helen and Newton Harrison.

There is a new institute within the University of Santa Cruz with 900 acres in the Sierras as a research lab. So the first step is to do research on what plants will be the best sponges, and how to move plants upland, and then create the variety of sponges that will hold the waters up in the mountains.

We are starting in the States – helping uplands adapt to climate change. Our first step may be to prepare patches of land from 8,000 to 14,000 feet up and do research on the evolution of the plants at these altitudes.

I have identified a Chinese scientist to work with us. This scientist, at Sichuan University, has been doing uplands for 20 years. And although there are many independent studies about the uplands, there has never been a sequential study, say for 10 years, about what would be appropriate flora and fauna to shift an ecosystem upland.

We need to learn to live together with the mountains, the hills, and the lowlands. We are all interdependent. We need to respect them. If you kill all of the mosquitoes, what will the birds eat? So we get bitten from time to time. Are we so superior that we have to eradicate them?

Betsy Damon on Hydro-fracking

In September 2012, I will be exhibiting an art project on the rules of water in Pittsburgh, Pennsylvania. I am going to have a map of what Pittsburgh was before it was Carnegie Mellon steel mills, and what it is now and what it could be if we let the water systems recover. I want to have an instant feedback with new technology for every hydro-fracking development that is going on in the surrounding areas.

The practice of hydraulic fracturing is a concern to many who live in the communities where fossil fuel is mined in this manner. The polluted water that goes into the rivers from the operation and the environmental damage are both quite extensive. These operations bring in money for the company and very little of it goes to the community since the work is highly technical. It has been suspended or banned in some countries.

How many billions of gallons of water are destroyed!? The main wastewater treatment plant in Pittsburgh has refused to take that water because they say that the water is so chemically dirty that they can't clean it up.

These kinds of people, who destroy the land and ruin the health of citizens because they want to make money, are no different from the feudal kings or the warlords from our global past. They just have different titles. However, it is perfectly possible, logical, and desirable that corporations become the leaders of resource responsibility, as sensibly, their future existence depends upon accessible resources.

Stephanie: Beijing is very concerned about food safety, and there is a growing demand for organic food and sustainable farming practices. There are a lot of Community Supported Agriculture (CSA) organizations around the world. Slow Food Movement, Farm to Fork, Farm to School. Some farmers are going back to traditional farming practices. There are also a growing number of community farms. Some are learning to farm all over again or enlarging their gardens so they don't have to buy so much food. In the U.S., unemployed people are going off to work organic farms for the room and board. Some young people are proactively going to farmers to learn how to farm so they can get back to the natural rhythms of nature.

Are these the growing pains for creating a sustainable city?

Betsy: I met the man who started CSA – he's a German, 80 years old when I met him. He started it right after the war. It was a tough time. People gave what they could. If they couldn't farm, they paid others to farm for them. Those people who didn't have money, came and farmed. It is hardship work. It doesn't actually work that way in the States.

My daughter is part of a CSA. She does all of the bookkeeping for a community garden – changing rubble into gardens has become a really big deal in Brooklyn, especially where we live.

There are some problems with old laws about what you can and cannot do to your yards. But that is changing now. In Portland you can now plant gardens as you like. We have legislated so much out what was once normal – like you can't hang your laundry out to dry. You can't be doing things the lower class might do. (*laughs and laughs*)

What a Sustainable City Would Be Like

Betsy: Cities need to live off their own footprint and sources as close to home as possible. City dwellers actually have smaller footprints than people who live in rural areas because they share such things as roads, electrical lines etc. More is shared in a city per person.

Waste treatments, the ones we now use, are so outdated because people think that larger is better. But there are many new inventions and technologies being developed. For example, buildings that can separate organic waste from other waste. Organic waste can be compacted, heated and made into dirt in four hours.

There is a kitchen waste treatment plant in operation in Beijing. Guozhong
Biotech sorts the garbage it receives. 60% is organic matter, 12% is plastic,
10% inorganic matter and 18 percent for everything else. A ton of rubbish
can produce 200 kilos of organic fertilizer, useful for agriculture and garden-
ing. The fertilizer costs around a quarter of the normal price. Many more
centers are adopting this technique. CCTV reporter Xue Jingmeng who
reported recently on this new method, said, "Much of our refuse could actu-
ally be put to good use, if efficient garbage treatment systems were available.
Re-using household waste must be an important component of any modern,
efficient and green economy." [1]

Many tons can be treated at once, with no pollution left over like we have
now. A waste treatment plant is central to a well-functioning community.
We now need to accept this reality.

In a sustainable city all buildings would separate toilet water from gray
water and reuse it for the gardens, toilets and roads. People would be conscious of what they toss into the waste systems. The cleared waste system
they use, and general waste as well. Some things would not be used – and
not allowed.

As much food as climate and circumstances permit needs to be produced
in or near the city. Every street would be tree-lined for climate mitiga-
tion. Buildings would have green roofs, and those needing screening,
could use green vertical growing gardens. People are designing these. I
know of some in New York. Imagine a sloping green wall so that each
floor has access to the green and can harvest from it. A building could be
green inside with grow lights and a glass roof. Although there are obvious
problems.

Public transport needs to be central and dominant. Many of the city spaces
should be auto-free. Electricity can be produced from renewables. This
could even replace old bulbs, which would reduce the energy load
immensely.

I don't like super-planned cities. However, if we did it, each square block of
half a million people, would have a waste treatment plant, hospital and elementary schools. Then some institutions would be shared with neighboring

blocks. People would live in diverse neighborhoods, so that all levels of social activity are mixed.

No one has to travel far to work, whether the working class, teachers or business people. Basically the structures of governance and protection would be such that there is not a huge difference in wealth. Our parks would be ecosystems, with wetlands that enable the land, air and water to revive.

When calculating the cost of doing this, we need to include the cost of flying food from elsewhere, the cost to the ecosystem of extracting, of building roads and other transportation, not just the single cost of building a more expensive structure. When we eat wrongly, the cost of the medical care to restore health needs to be calculated into the cost to the ecosystem.

Plastic never goes away – the ocean – 40% has been plasticized. The blood in fish is about 60% plasticized. So, plastic is not a sustainable solution for cities.

Sustainable City Means Ensuring Water Sustainability

Each city, every city, needs to live off its water footprint. That means their water comes from the rainfall that falls on the city plus the aquifers underneath the city. This may sound impossible.

However, if a city were to separate the drinking water supply from all others needs and then carefully source their drinking waters from pristine sources, reuse the gray water, and have many small wastewater treatment plants district by district, use all of the effluent, and have public drinking fountains, most cities would be able to sustain themselves on their natural nearby water sources. Extraction of water sources for bottling or to feed cities is bad. They eventually destroy valuable ecosystems on which a city lives, upon which we all live.

In your home, your drinking water supply is primary. So put a filter in it. In your community, the wastewater treatment plants should be as important as the hospital. It can be an asset that is green and productive.

Municipalities want to use chemicals so they are absolutely sure there are no pathogens, but then those chemicals get released into the environment. We need to make sure these chemicals are limited. We know how to do this so there is no smell. You don't need a lot of chemicals and the chemicals can be made to disappear in the final processing. These plants can become an amenity.

If you really want to talk about a sustainable city, you've got to talk about this wastewater treatment. Organic waste into fertilizer. Water treated to become pristine again. This is the direction that new technology needs to continue to move in.

China is renowned for being able to produce food on the same land for centuries. Now we need a modern way to do this. CURA in Chengdu is developing the use of separation toilets, for example. China and the world can create completely integrated food and waste systems for cities. I have great expectations that China understands the vital importance of this. I really think that China could lead the way here.

Beijing as a Sustainable Society

Sustainable Development Structure in China and Beijing

China's National Development and Reform Commission, a part of the State Council, has the responsibility to make economic plans for China, as well as supervise and direct the development of China's economy. It is also responsible for promoting the strategy of sustainable development, including energy saving and emission reduction, developing a recycling economy, and protecting the environment.

Beijing has its Municipal Commission of Development and Reform. Each of the districts has a commission as well. It is here where the structure for a sustainable city must and is being constructed. Beijing's Master Plan is set up with the goal, among others, of becoming a livable city by 2020. It is creating satellite cities to ease resources. Landscaping that can also function as sustainability systems is part of this plan. Thanks to the continuous dialogue in cyberspace between netizens, government and experts, there is a growing agreement that Beijing needs to change.

There are many local NGOs that support specific areas of urban sustainability and work together with local governments and the municipality. Civil society is young in China and many are still sorting out how best to cooperate with a government that has so much more power. Getting this relationship right so that collaboration happens is the work the municipal government must take on. You can't get to a sustainable society without heartfelt cooperation.

The people most involved are professionals – government experts and academics, business and industry. They know that with resources so limited, it is becoming socially irresponsible not to be doing something that is helpful.

The rest of Beijingers work at other things – students, manual labor, white collar workers, housekeepers, merchants, teachers, taxi drivers or getting their children into good schools. They all endure the crowds, noise and the smog.

Beijing is a long way from a sustainable city. A vast amount of water now has to come from hundreds of kilometers away. The air is so bad that netizens were able to force Beijing Municipality to install proper measuring devices. The soil is deeply damaged by chemical fertilizers. Can this city become a good place to live in the future? It is hard for anyone to have hope.

What will it take to make the impossible possible? Will a genius just show up? Will the Eight Immortals save the day? Will Huangdi come and show us the way? Who can we turn to?

Creating Good Soil

Lu Xun, in a speech to the Middle School of Beijing Normal University in 1924, said that rather than wait for a genius to appear, we should all become good soil and grow some geniuses. You can't grow beans from sprouts on a plate. You need good soil.

Of course the soil cannot be compared with genius, but even to be the soil is difficult unless we persevere and spare no pains. Still, everything depends on men's efforts, and here we have a better chance of success than if we wait idly for a heaven-sent genius. In this lies the strength of the soil and its great expectations, as well as its reward. For when a beautiful blossom grows from the soil, all who see it naturally take pleasure in the sight, including the soil itself. [1]

Lu Xun's China was closed to much of the world. Today it is not. Who can fertilize the "soil" of Beijing? Give the energy required for new growth? Who will help "water," the vortex, begin to move? Who can make this city become a good place to live in the future?

Nine Beijingers have addressed these questions and answered them for themselves. We can say that they have recovered their heart.

Mac Fan is energized about food safety. From someone concerned mostly with feeding his family by being a good businessman, he grew into someone who is actively helping his fellow citizens understand about food safety and how to care for the land. He knows just what to say to get them to really listen.

Within the algorithm that is Little Donkey Farm, Yan Xiaohui found his home in the James Yen Institute and began to fuse his life and acumen with Huang Zhiyou and his deep respect for the soil and Yuan Qinghua's struggle to connect with the heart in the farmer. And with the rest of the Every-humans at the farm, together with the land, they are forging a new idea, a way to reveal the true relationship between the farmer and the urban citizen. You could say that they are nurturing soil citizens who synergize with nature.

He Huili used the lessons she learned in Beijing to reconfigure creating the same right relationships between citizen and farmer in Henan, so that the future of the villages of her home district and now her province is better for all. At the same time her struggles in Beijing gave her the experience and wisdom to help citizen cooperatives develop, help students develop their own passion to resolve the urban/rural divide, and send out support to organic ventures.

Yang Ke's contribution to how to make this city a good place to live is growing soil through her public platform with netizens. This brings in fresh ideas for the municipality to explore and asks for wisdom from the Beijing public. She also provides insight into the role or function of communication in creating the desire to build better consensus and community. Jim Spear adds a riff on the vital integration of creative urban design and wellbeing. He also addresses the value of the authentic in providing long-term livelihoods and wellbeing.

Wang Zhiqin fuses of tradition and the new into a dance of life, so people in her community can become conscious about the nature around them while pursuing their common interests and friendships. Yang Jing's young passion for play, led to sport kiting and an exhilarating way to connect to nature. He also provides a window for others to realize that their own future depends on opening their minds too, which he provides through his website.

Zhang Zhimin's existential struggle is creating new good soil. She has recaptured the depths of her traditional Chinese sustainable life philosophy and coupled it with international practices. Betsy Damon leads the same kind of existential life, at the beginning providing Beijing with some of its first lessons in real sustainable urban planning. More recently she designed the wetlands of Olympic Forest Park, providing an ongoing source of fresh air and water. Each of these nine valiant *junzi* is a testimony that Beijingers can recover their hearts and get in the game too.

Beijing needs to coalesce into a sustainable society. The municipal governments cannot do this alone. To become such a society, city dwellers have to *want* to live in a sustainable society. Beijing can become a sustainable society if we all do our part.

Beijing Is a Part of Nature

What is a society then? There are many definitions, but the one I like is by the educator Tsunesaburo Makiguchi (1861-1944), who said that a society consists of various individuals just as a living body consists of various cells. It has a common purpose, which members hold to consciously or unconsciously. The members willingly contribute to the welfare of the whole. There is a permanent mental or spiritual relationship between the individual members of a society and they live connected to a particular geographic area.

Perhaps Beijingers don't quite feel a permanent mental or spiritual relationship with one another. Most of them weren't here sixty years ago. However, since many of the city residents want to stay, Beijingers need to decide to be a society. And to consider the plain beneath our feet our home.

Cities are part of nature too. Nature abounds with different kinds of societies – herds, anthills, schools of fish, flocks of birds. We need to remember that even when we live in this artificial jungle, that no life form can create matter. Every bit of the city is something we have only shaped, not created. All of us are beholden to the soil to feed us and the planet and the larger universe to create the matter we need in our lives. To continue to be so ignorant of this is perilous.

On the other hand, we can evolve and develop our consciousness, so we can make better use of the matter we have. We can consciously decide to appreciate nature. To show our gratitude to nature, we can decide to lend our support to the city's effort to become sustainable. Jim Spear consciously created a business that also provides meaningful livelihoods for the local villagers. This revitalizes the nature around him and his guests, He Huili consciously decided to take on the rural-city divide, and works night and day on her passion. Working at what Jim and He Huili loves best. How great is that!

A sustainable society is one where there is a healthy relationship between the whole and the individual. *In a healthy community citizens want to contribute.* Each citizen plays an important role – to connect his or her avocation, what he or she most loves to work on, and apply it to the concerns of the common community. We, as a community, may not be healthy now, but such intentional actions will certainly begin the cure.

Connect the Functions of the City Back to Nature, Naturally

Makiguchi said there is nothing wrong with having cities, industry, and businesses. Indeed they perform a vital role in a society. Do we all want to make bread every morning? Do you want to design and put a vehicle together, create its energy source, decide the regulations for driving, and pave the roads so you can drive it to see your friends in the next province? I don't think so.

The problem is just that so many of the functions in the city are out of balance. But if they are recalibrated so all the wheels are aligned, like in a car, they will all grip the road at the same time, and the ride will become smoother.

Our daily lives are carried out within a social and environment platform. We do different things. We are farmers, government workers, scholars, teachers, police, priests, entrepreneurs, laborers – all according to our individual skills and desires. We cooperate, compete and develop more and more complex ways to do these things. But we all do them in the city and what we do impacts others. So first, we need to recognize our mutual interdependence and work together, just like the ears, eyes, hands, legs and our brain in a body, work together in the overall interests of that body. The right relationship between self and other creates prosperity. Bad relationships create problems. We can work on our own right relationships. Then the functions of the city will start to rebalance. Not because of a miracle, but because nature is all about being in balance.

Waste management and wastewater management function as a barometer of transformation now. Deciding what you can do so your home is more sustainable is a great interdependent action to take. Mac Fan, Betsy Damon and Yang Ke may not always agree, but they serve as lanterns in the dark here helping build the tipping point when everyone begins to do his or her part. Beijing can become a recycling queen. Indeed, Betsy will say that our very future depends on this darkest of matter. Buddhists say that the most beautiful lotuses grow from the dirtiest swamps. The day should come when the water in our city is alive again. This will mean that our city is truly a sustainable one.

The functions of business and industry are to provide a means to make a living. They have however created many of our social and environmental problems, because they changed our basic relationship with nature. The primary industries of agriculture, fishing, and clothing materials all had direct contact with nature. Today many people, white and blue collar workers alike, are completely cut off from such direct contact.

Because industry has the power to provide what people want and need, it also has the power to override the reign of nature in human affairs. We prefer to buy instant food because we are busy. We need washable clothes because we can't afford help and we don't want to iron. In pursuit of cash, both parents work in such industries, and must save for the university; so little time is spent raising children, many of whom are raised by their grandparents. Being oblivious about our connection with nature though only makes things worse.

So industry and business must recalibrate for the public good as well as for their own bottom line. Many are already doing so. Much work needs to be done. The sustainable consumer can do a lot to move them in the right direction. Choose to buy wisely. Choose to buy healthy. Work where volunteerism is appreciated. What people want to buy is *the* barometer for Apple. Why not for others? Business and industry are listening.

The function of governance is to provide the security, education, policies, economic and housing oversight with an eye towards the future. This means that the city must find the right balance between the needs of the people and the industries and institutions that provide livelihoods. This is not easy. The municipality wants to provide more nature per city resident in the future but making it happen will take better collaboration with the public and with the other functions in the city. Again interdependent consciousness is very useful here. We can help make this a reality.

As Zhang Zhimin said, hard work is very satisfying. It feels good to labor at work that provides for ourselves and family and also contributes in a healthy way to society. Such a society can evolve only when there is collaboration and integration between livelihoods and the respect for the dignity of life for all life forms. Between what your work is and the nature you use to do it.

We could all learn a lesson or two from Zhang Zhimin and her biodynamic farm, from the Brickyard or Little Donkey Farm. They all took damaged land or impoverished human resources and nurtured them back to health. Why can't we integrate back into the land? Then the birds will serenade us. Our employees will praise us. And industry will have the reward they seek but have yet to find – a sustainable income for everyone for the foreseeable future so people can buy their products for a long time to come.

We need to remind ourselves that it is we, laborers in business, industry and trade, who are, with the sweat of our brows, either on the land or in the office, are the means for future prosperity for all. It is the very act of working. Why? Because there are so many of us and we all expend energy to do this work. Change why we work and the world changes too. Not a miracle just an example of how interdependence works.

Jim Spear's sustainable tourism and his relationship with his local villages are great examples of energy well spent. Yang Jing, in his own way, is a chef who, in his spare time, creates symbiosis with nature on weekends. Wang Zhiqin was an engineer working on coal resources and now chooses to spend time dancing with nature and her friends. All this energy is helping recreate balance.

Finally, we need to address this vital fair trade relationship between city and the rural community that supports it. This relationship needs to be recognized as a necessity for a sustainable city, and part of its interdependent reality. Indeed, neither is complete without the other.

We can neither afford the decline of the primary industries, which come for the rural community, nor the decline of our industries because of lack of resources. The health of Beijingers and Beijing itself is jeopardized when the productivity of the land and vital resources is sacrificed. The city is essential and but it needs to operate in balance with nature.

As a society, creating lines of communication between the functions and sectors is essential as each separate entity rebalances its particular relationship with nature and human society.

Here the skill at dialogue is very helpful. Not by herding cats, but by collaborating and finding meaningful ways to help one another. This is what creates synergy.

Little Donkey Farm can be seen, at a micro level, to have shaped its functions and sectors and directed them towards a sustainable society. They learned first to work respectfully with the farmers even when the farmers didn't appreciate it. They located a nexus point between themselves as activists and the farmers. They created consumer cooperatives, and invited communication that directly connected the farmer to the city resident through the farming plots. They drive into the city to pick-up points, but also people like to come out to the farm and work with the farmers. They created meetings and relationships between farmers and residents where the foundation of the relationship is to work together towards sustainable living and eating. In a tiny way you can see the seeds of a sustainable society. How did they do it? By rebalancing the relationships of the functions of the small community they have. Probably impossible without the deepening connection to the land by all of them.

An Awakening in Education that Begins with Contact with Nature

The Everyhumans in this book are a product of globalization, new ideas and a desire to live an authentic life. Each of them abandoned a normal education or career to venture out to solve an issue he or she is passionate about. Not the life that is normally thought about in the halls of ministries of education around the world.

How did education get so off track that it doesn't serve the sustainable needs of human society, which is part of nature? Lifelong sustainable education, both informal and formal, can rectify this.

Public education around the world is less than 200 years old. During its first century education was centered on nationalism and citizenship. More recently it has been about developing a society that will consume what the market economy sells.

Machiavelli wrote that societies that are controlled by fear eventually collapse and ones supported by compassion and wisdom endure. We saw that fear factor develop most recently with the War in Iraq when the neo-realist gang created a false fear which consumed millions of lives and billions of dollars and led to an internationally disgraced and impoverished American society. Or the fear created by the Gang of Four that consumed Chinese people during the Cultural Revolution, where even family members turned on one another to save their own lives. Education did nothing to avert these two disasters. Nor does it create the care that enables the right kind of society to emerge.

Why does education take so much of the lives of young people, and then fail at helping people live meaningful lives? This is because it is disconnected from nature. Math, sciences, language arts are only taught as information. No time is given to understanding how they help students live life wisely. To help develop experience in real life and explore and understand the world. To help them practice developing great relationships with other humans and nature.

For example, Wang Zhiqin learned only in retirement an exercise that brings her happiness, and also enables her to help others too. It took a performance artist, Betsy Damon, to help the mayor of Chengdu figure out that cleaning up his polluted river was a possibility. Only 60 years ago, artisans were washing their famous brocade cloth in the same water. Harmony with nature is a natural solution for a sustainable city.

Chinese curriculum is an amalgamation of traditional, socialist and Western educational systems. There already exists a sustainable development curriculum, like other curricula in the world, and it is mostly information. Effort now, is being made to include Chinese traditional values such as balance.

In addition to this new focus, a program that connects students to nature should be inserted, at the beginning of children's education to help them connect what they will be learning to nature and the community they live in. This would connect all of the rest of their education to their living community and help students organize what they learn so it is useful to them. Then you will start to have a society that learns to connect directly to real life.

These nine Everyhumans learned to live authentic lives on their own. Yan Xiaohui left his university because it wasn't a place where he could work on a way to save nature. Jim Spear had a midlife crisis, and this led to a life of contribution to his guests, the villagers and the land. Zhang Zhimin couldn't find something to eat in the new supermarkets and so decided on a life of struggle. She can now enjoy her home on the land where birds come to sing to her.

Don't we all want to have meaningful lives? These people have organized their world in such a way through using their experiences to guide them. Their lives showed them their next steps. They sought a conjunction with the universe around them. They used the math, the science, the art, their traditions, their language and their sense of community to further their goals. Through their own direct observation, they learned how to comprehend strategies that align with nature and society. They can discern both the artificial and natural reality. Then they apply this to planning future action. We all can do this.

Education should serve people and help them want to live a sustainable life, support their community, and know and do the right thing. Then naturally the students will want to give back their community. To help their dear community that nourished them. When giving back to your community becomes natural again will be a sign that our species is evolving.

Creating the Right Relationship with Power

What prevents common people from wanting to contribute to a society? This is the most fundamental question for the future of humanity.

Perhaps we are not yet evolved to that state. Yet neo-evolutionists say that humanity has arrived at a new stage – that we are endeavoring to be a collaborative species.

Other scientists have discovered that we are hardwired, not to compete, but to empathize with fellow humans and other forms of life. Perhaps, then, it is education that must change. Away from nurturing the kind of competition that steps on others who get in the way, or where personal desires override moral values. Towards humanitarian competition, where people compete to bring more value to their community and in this way to the world.

For these reasons, it is important to address the role of power. We are not taught enough about the complex and multiple dimensions of power in the natural world and in human affairs, and how to grow and progress by building sound relationships. Something every cub in a wolf pack knows.

Power that is active, suppressive and directive has an important impact on a child because it is experienced through all the senses. Senses are how we evaluate and learn from the world around us. How we deal with such power determines our future. Because it is not taught in school, when students experience such power, they don't have a way to talk about it, even though their human dignity and potential are at stake. Those, through chance, who have been able to organize their thinking about it, learn to use their skill at relationships to turn encounters with such power into medicine for their growth. They maintain their dignity. Human dignity enables people to live a contributive life.

If students grow up comfortable with the life around them, they feel a natural desire to support that life with their own. We misunderstood survival of the fittest to mean most physically fit, instead of most able to be an important part of the human community. The West went towards individualism and the east towards harmony. What we need to be in the Mean – is to discover our right way to act, based on our perception at the moment. To be conscious about what is the right thing to do. That consciousness comes from the wisdom we accumulate through the relationships we experiences in life.

Our nine friends all have become conscious through the relationships they developed and experienced. Mac Fan by helping Beijingers eat mindfully. He Huili by helping reduce the rural/urban gap. Yang Ke by creating an open space where citizens can choose to act wisely rather than be told or fined into compliance. They have learned to create the right dialogue with power and to act with their heart.

Students should be able to become aware of all life forms in their environment, and to live conscious of the beautiful and mystic universal relationships around him. To live in an interdependent universe. Also to recognize that living things disperse and integrate and have an influence on us at some points but not at others. Because these living things in our environment have their own life stories. The ants on the beach that you are lying on, are only temporarily engaged in eating your tuna sandwich, which infuriates you, for example. Later they will go about their own lives and so will you. If you can recognize and respect their right to their own story, you will see how their patterns connect with yours, and this will enable you to see how to work with life. The ants don't like cayenne pepper. Sprinkling it around your picnic site is like Zhang Zhimin dealing with her aphids in a respectful way. Do they really deserve to die because you brought tuna fish into their territory?

Such simple acts that recognize we live in an interconnected community – with members of our species and other life – are acts of consciousness. Conscious living enables us, as Abraham Maslow showed us, to live a contributive life. We *are* hardwired to be empathic, to have compassion, to be wise. By correcting the imbalances created by education systems around the world that feed off each other's imbalances, we can then raise human beings who understand and hold dear the community that nurtured them. Like the wolf pup who learns to become part of a pack, we can take our right place in our community and gladly participate in nourishing our community. We can then feel the harmony in our blood and contribute to it.

The Art and Power of Dialogue

The power of dialogue is not suppressive. It is empowering. We are very weak at dialogue at present but in fact dialogue has tremendous power. Think of Lu Xun, Gandhi, Jesus, Mohammed, Confucius. Why are there so few great people who speak and the world listens? I think it is because we don't realize that we all have the same incredible potential. We don't realize we can consciously grow our relationships. If we can start to develop our own dialogue skills, we can participate in the dialogue that will create a sustainable society.

Every relationship is either an I/It one or an I/Thou one. An I/It relationship is one where you use that person or the other person uses you. Like Yang Jing spoke about with his kite. If you think the other person is just a toy for you to use or discard for your own benefit, then that is your relationship. If you use water to make money, you can easily use people to make your quarterly financial goals.

I/Thou relationships, on the other hand, are those where you and that Other Person, deeply respect and care about each other. Your wonderful relationship with your mother, for example, your best friend, your soul mate, your God, or your business, your ship or your home. For example, going home means more than to get to a house that you own or rent. It is where your family is, or where your heart is. This is how Farmer Zhang feels about her farm. Betsy about water. Jim about the Mutianyu community. Yan about living his dream.

The I/Thou can be very slow and not every It can be changed at once into a Thou. But such dialogue enables the soul to emerge. The rewards are deep and the satisfaction with life an eternal reality. It takes time to create but it is so illuminating.

Dialogue is not manipulation, like with Hitler, or political parties who will do and say anything to get your vote. Or ads and salespeople to get your money. The art of dialogue comes from your character and respect for the Other. When Mac talks about safe food, people are influenced because he is a man of character, and you see he feels deeply for his countrymen. It is not always what you want to hear. Jim Spear, though he loves his country, speaks sincerely about his admiration of certain policies and perspectives of the Chinese government. You may or may not agree with his opinion but you respect him. Dialogue is harmony through diversity. Harmony is only obtained through creating collaboration from truly diverse viewpoints. Wonderful!

Governments are rarely good at dialogue with their citizens. Governments are always trying to teach us, inform us or threaten us for our own good. Citizens seldom trust governments. So, if we wait for authorities to find the right way to engage our support, Beijing will never become a sustainable city.

The same is true about industry and business. It is only the naive who believe that material wealth will bring happiness. Unsustainable consumption will only make us destitute.

If we wait for experts and professionals, again the same is true. At NSCL we once asked the environment officer from the U.S. Embassy to talk to students. He said that the sustainable development community is not good at communicating to people about the environmental crisis and they need our help. People-to-people is a much more effective way of creating collaboration. In the end, as Yuan Qingua discovered with his farmers, real relationships are what really count here. NOT the law. We city folk just forgot about that.

The Beijing Municipality is listening. Not all the time, or well enough probably. And the citizens are right to be angry and frustrated. Don't stop there, Everyhumans. Make right happen. Create connections in your own small community and you will affect the rest of the city. You will become part of the vortex that is creating the change.

As good example of an important contribution by the Beijing Municipality is Olympic Forest Park. Created by the Beijing Tsinghua Urban Planning and Design Institute, with the help of Betsy Damon, this is a very successful and biodynamic park in north of Beijing, near the Bird's Nest. Designed using the traditional *shanshui* (Mountain-Water or urban design using natural topography) design with modern advances and Betsy's living water principles, this is an authentic sustainable urban park. It includes wetlands, canals, waterfalls, a large lake for boating and skating, bird sanctuary, a geothermal heating system for buildings, cultural venues for theater and dance, and landscaping that invites water to create a natural ecosystem. It is integrated into the surrounding urban landscape in such a way that it has many visitors. People are there every day, enjoying spending time with their friends there and walking or jogging along the pathways. Combining tradition with sound sustainable and innovative elements, the park resonates well with the values needed for a sustainable society and truly enjoyed by the citizens. Beijingers can come to value living a sustainable way of life.

We can decide to sort our garbage, reduce our use of plastic, and start changing our relationships for the better. We will be changing the future with every such action. We can take up a passion and pursue it. Or consciously take walks in the park and admire the nature around us, or pursue an outdoor activity and take moments for some gratitude for the planet. These are relations that interconnect us with all of life.

The universe interconnects through thoughts, words and deeds. Each of us can become the conductor of a magnificent symphony. Our nine Everyhumans are already communing musically with the cosmos on this plain that is Beijing. We, like they, can recover our hearts and become part of the future sustainable Beijing too. Those outside Beijing can help by working on their own cities. We are one human family after all.

What a piece of work is a man! How noble in reason! How infinite in faculties! In form and moving how express and admirable! In action how like an angel! In apprehension how like a god! The beauty of the world! The paragon of animals!

Beijing Olympic
Forest Park

Resources

International

United Nations Environment Programme Urban Environment Unit
http://www.unep.org/urban_environment/key_programmes/index.asp

China

National Development and Reform Commission
http://en.ndrc.gov.cn

Ministry of Environmental Protection (English Website)
http://english.mep.gov.cn

Beijing Municipality

Beijing Municipal Environmental Protection Bureau
http://ebeijing.gov.cn (English); www.bjee.com.cn (Chinese)

Beijing Municipal Commission of Development and Reform
http://www.bjpo.gov.cn/english

Beijing Haidian District Development and Reform Commission
http://www.hddrc.gov.cn/en

Beijing Chaoyang District Development and Reform Commission (Chinese version only)
http://fagaiwei.bjchy.gov.cn

Beijing Dongcheng District Development and Reform Commission (Chinese version only)
http://fzjhw.bjdch.gov.cn/n5687274/n5723019/index.html

Beijing Xicheng District Development and Reform Commission (see Beijing Municipality) Beijing Fengtai District Development and Reform Commission (website in development)
http://fgw.bjft.gov.cn

Beijing Daxing District Development and Reform Commission (Chinese version only)
http://dxfg.bjdx.gov.cn/web/fgw

Beijing Everyhumans

Betsy Damon
Keepers of the Waters
http://www.keepersofthewaters.org

and
Chengdu Urban Rivers Association
http://www.org.cn/jigojieshao/guanyuwomen/200903/48.html
and
HU Jie
Beijing Olympic Park
Beijing Tsinghua Urban Planning and Design Institute
www.thupdi.com

He Huili
China Agriculture University
www.cau.edu.cn/cie/en; www.crcop.com

Jim Spear
The Schoolhouse at Mutianyu
http://www.theschoolhouseatmutianyu.com

Little Donkey Farm
www.littledonkeyfarm.com

Mac Fan (FAN Minjian)
Jane Goodall Institute in China
http://www.jgichina.org

Wang Zhiqin
www.earthchartercommunitiesnetwork.com

Yang Ke
Center for Environmental Education and Communications
Ministry of Environmental Protection (English Website)
http://english.mep.gov.cn

Zhang Zhimin (Therese)
God's Green Garden
tfyjlb@sina.com

Sustainable Cities Organizations

Sustainable Cities
http://sustainablecities.dk

Sustainable Cities International
http://sustainablecities.net

Welcome to Sustania
http://greengrowthleaders.org/wp-content/uploads/2011/10/GUIDE-TO-SUSTAINIA.pdf

Glossary

Biodynamic agriculture is a method of organic farming that emphasizes the holistic development and interrelationships of the soil, plants and animals as a self-sustaining system. Biodynamic farming has much in common with other organic approaches, such as emphasizing the use of manures and composts and excluding of the use of artificial chemicals on soil and plants. There are independent certification agencies for bio-dynamic products; most of these agencies are members of the international biodynamic standards group, Demeter International. Biodynamics originated out of the work of Rudolf Steiner, the founder of anthroposophy.

Community-Supported Agriculture, a form of an alternative food network, (in Canada Community Shared Agriculture) (CSA) is a socio-economic model of agriculture and food distribution. A CSA consists of a community of individuals who pledge support to a farming operation where the growers and consumers share the risks and benefits of food production. CSAs usually have a system of weekly delivery or pick-up of vegetables and fruit, in a vegetable box scheme, and sometimes including dairy products and meat.

Datong (大同) Huangdi, the father of Chinese civilization, had a dream. In the dream he saw an ideal kingdom develop in the future where peaceful descendants would live in harmonious accord with the natural law. Waking from his dream, Huangdi named this Datong (The Great Harmony). He sought to inculcate this in his kingdom to ensure order and prosperity for his people. The people made him an Immortal. This story has been handed down generation after generation for these 5,000 years. This is still taught to most children in China today, although today, it is a distant ideal at best, and is fading.

Desertification is the degradation of land in any dry land. Caused by a variety of factors, such as climate change and human activities, desertification is one of the most significant global environmental problems.

Huangdi (黄帝) is the father of Chinese civilization. Although some believe that he is just a figurehead that embodies important ideas, inventions and the stability that enabled the Chinese to flourish, he is said to have lived 5,000 years ago. He and Shennong, the father of Chinese agriculture, were contemporaries in some way.

Humanitarian competition is the idea first proposed by Tsunesaburo Makiguchi that we need to evolve beyond military and economic competition that is based on survival of the fittest, and develop the capacity to compete for the betterment of oneself and society. Polishing your own capabilities but also helping others develop their own expertise and success. This provides the development of a future where everyone prospers.

Junzi (君子) comes from the teachings of Confucius. To be *junzi* means to be an exemplary person, who knows and can do the right thing. A truly *junzi* person can do this each moment. We all have the potential to do this without exception. We just don't believe that we are capable of this, so we don't try and develop the self-mastery it takes. But if we just start, we can become *junzi* little by little. The more you do the right thing, the more your character evolves into a person who does this intrinsically.

Liang Shuming (1893-1988) was a philosopher, teacher, and leader in the Rural Reconstruction Movement in the late Qing Dynasty and early Republican eras of Chinese history. Liang was of Guilin, Guangxi origin, but born in Beijing. He had a modern Chinese and Western education and mixed this with Confucianism, Henry Bergson and Buddhist Yogacara.

Loess Plateau, also known as the **Huangtu Plateau**, is a plateau that covers an area of some 640,000 km² in the upper and middle reaches of China's

Yellow River. Loess is the name for the silty sediment that has been deposited by windstorms on the plateau over the ages. Loess is a highly erosion-prone soil that is susceptible to the forces of wind and water; in fact, the soil of this region has been called the "most highly erodible soil on earth." The Loess Plateau and its dusty soil cover almost all of Shanxi and Shaanxi provinces, as well as parts of Gansu province, Ningxia Hui Autonomous Region, and Inner Mongolia Autonomous Region.

Monoculture is the agricultural practice of producing or growing one single crop over a wide area. It is also known for the farming practice of growing large stands of a single species. It is widely used in modern industrial agriculture and its implementation has allowed large harvests from minimal labor. However, this ratio remains true only if the accounting for labor required is limited to the number of workers employed on the farm. If the indirect work of employees involved in producing chemicals and machinery are taken into account, the ratio of labor to output is higher. Monocultures can lead to the quicker spread of diseases. "Crop monoculture" is the practice of growing the same crop year after year.

Netizen, a word combination of Internet and citizen, is a person who is actively involved in online communities, especially in regard to open access to information and free speech.

Sustainable society means one where people experience wellbeing, cooperate with one another, are happy about their lives, have meaningful livelihoods, and are sustainable consumers. Such a society, its politics and economy, are not GDP-centered but rather concentrates on the development of community.

Sustainable tourism is tourism attempting to make a low impact on the environment and local culture, while helping to generate future employment for local people. The aim of sustainable tourism is to ensure that development brings a positive experience for local people, tourism companies and the tourists themselves. Sustainable tourism is not the same as ecotourism.

Wen Tiejun (dean of the School of Agricultural Economics and Rural Development at Renmin University) developed the phrase *"sannong wenti"* (three rural problems), that is, *nongmin* (rural people or peasants), *nongcun* (rural society or villages), and *nongye* (rural production or agriculture). According to Wen's theory, Mao-era policies such as economic independence from the world capitalist system were necessary for China to industrialize, but these policies left the rural population in a weak position. To solve these contradictions, further market reforms were not the right strategy. Rural life needs to be reconstructed. A people-centered scientific approach and sustainable development is the correct solution. His James Yen Institute laid the foundation for Little Donkey Farm.

Y.C. James Yen (or Yen Yangchu, 1890-1990) is a Chinese educator and organizer who in the 1920s first organized the Mass Education Movement to bring literacy to the Chinese masses, then turned to the villages of China to organize rural reconstruction, most famously at Ding Xian, a county in Hebei, from 1926-1937. After 1949, Dr. Yen organized the Philippine Rural Reconstruction Movement and the International Institute of Rural Reconstruction. He returned to China in the 1980s but died in New York in 1990.

Vortex (*plural:* vortices) is a spinning, often turbulent, flow of fluid. Any spiral motion with closed streamlines is vortex flow. The motion of the fluid swirling rapidly around a center is called a vortex. The speed of the fluid in a free (irrotational) vortex is greatest at the center, and decreases progressively with distance from the center, whereas the speed of a forced (rotational) vortex is zero at the center and increases proportional to the distance from the center.

Notes

Introduction

1. 侯仁之 (Hou Renzhi),《北京城的生命印记》(北京 : 生活读书新知三联书店 , 2009) 65.

2. 侯仁之 , 4.

3. 侯仁之 , 5.

4. 侯仁之 , 6.

5. 侯仁之 , 10.

6. 侯仁之 , 12.

7. Edwin O Reischauer, John K. Fairbank, *East Asia The Great Tradition* (Boston: Houghton Mifflin, 1958), 38.

8. Reischauer and Fairbank, *East Asia*, 38.

9. Ibid., 48-52.

10. Tu Weiming and Daisaku Ikeda, *New Horizons in Eastern Humanism; Buddhism, Confucianism and the Quest for Global Peace* (London: I.B. Tauris, 2011), 60.

11. E.R. Hughes, ed., trans., *Chinese Philosophy in Classical Times*

(London: J.M. Dent & Sons, 1942, reprinted 1960), 32.

12. Xu Yuanzhong, translated, versified, and annotated, *Book of Songs* (Beijing: China Literature Press 1994,) 29.

13. Reischauer and Fairbank, 73.

14. Tu Weiming and Daisaku Ikeda, 62.

15. T. Colin Campbell and Thomas M. Campbell II, *The China Study* (Dallas: Benbella Books: 2006), 344-5.

16. Campbell and Campbell, 345.

Chapter One: Mac Fan

1. E.R. Hughes, 39.

Chapter Two: Little Donkey Farm

1. 寇延丁，"黄志友：赤脚走在土地上"，《一切从改变自己开始》(海口：海南出版社，2007), 203.

2. 寇延丁，"严晓辉：找到属于自己的路"《一切从改变自己开始》(海 口：海南出版社，2007), 205.

3. 寇延丁，"袁清华：摸索困惑与失落之间，"《一切从改变自己开始》(海口：海南出版社，2007), 218.

4. Reischauer and Fairbank,159.

5. Xie Chuntao, ed. *Why and How the CPC Works in China* (Beijing: New World Press, 2011), 9.

6. 寇延丁，"严晓辉：找到属于自己的路"《一切从改变自己开始》(海口：海南出版社，2007), 210.

Chapter Three: Yang Ke

1. 北京生活垃圾产生量惊人 厨房废弃物成减量重点，北京晚报，2010-04-24.

2. 北京垃圾管理走向何方—访中国社科院城市发展与环境研究所副研究员李宇军，城市管理与科技，2010/3.

3. 北京 1200 个垃圾分类试点小区改用可降解垃圾袋，北京日报，2011-08-17.

4. 北京西城：紧锣密鼓采购环卫车，中国政府采购报，2011-08-15.

5. 垃圾分类指导员王凤琴："看见垃圾桶就特亲切"人民日报，2011-08-25.

6. 垃圾分类指导员王凤琴："看见垃圾桶就特亲切"，人民日报，2011-08-25.

Chapter Five: He Huili

1. Simon Hoiberg Olsen, presentation slide at IGES Conference at Beijing Normal University, December 2010.

Chapter Six: Wang Zhiqin

1. Ni, Yan. "The relationship between the nature and human reflected in Taiji softball." Report. Beijing Normal University. Aug. 28, 2011.1.

2. Ni, Yan. 2.

Chapter Seven: Zhang Zhimin

1. Zhang Zhimin. "Insects Are The Messengers of the Nature." Trans. Yan Ni. Zhang Zhimin's Blog. 24 Jan. 2010. 4 Aug. 2011 http://blogs.bnet.com.cn/?uid-3633-action-viewspace-itemid-8529.

Chapter Eight: Yang Jing

1. Hongmei Lu and Dongmei Lu, *Beijing at Play* (Beijing: China Intercontinental Press, 2008), 15.

2. Http://en.wikipedia.org/wiki/Sport_kite (3 April 2012).

Chapter Nine: Betsy Damon

1. CCTV.CN May 16 (Xinhuanet) "Turning waste into fertilizer" http://news.xinhuanet.com/english2010/video/2011-05/16/c_12877203.htm. Accessed Dec. 15, 2011.

Chapter Ten: Beijing as a Sustainable Society

1. Lu Xun, *Waiting for a Genius*, www.marxists.org/archive/lu-xun/1924/01/17.htm. Accessed Nov. 25, 2011.

Credits for Illustrations

005 "Peking Man" @ 2008 by Mutt, used under a Creative Commons Attribution-Share Alike license: http://creativecommons.org/licenses/by-sa/3.0/

005 "Zhoukoudian Upper Cave" @ 2006 by Mutt, used under a Creative Commons Attribution-Share Alike license: http://creativecommons.org/licenses/by-sa/3.0/

006 "Bronze Steamer" @ 2006 by PENG Yanan (Neo-Jay), used under a Creative Commons Attribution-Share Alike 3.0 Alike 3.0 Unported license.

006 "Yan State Coins" @ 2008 by PENG Yanan (Neo-Jay), used under a Creative Commons Attribtion-Share Alike license: http://creativecommons.org/licenses/by-sa/3.0/

008 "Niujie Mosque" @ 2006 by smartneddy, used under a Creative Commons Attribution-Share Alike 2.5 Generic license: http://creativecommons.org/licenses/by-sa/2.5/

图书在版编目（CIP）数据

心灵的回归：北京的未来在你我手中：英文 /
（美）坦西著. --北京：新世界出版社，2012.4
ISBN 978-7-5104-2634-6

Ⅰ.①心… Ⅱ.①坦… Ⅲ.①人物－访问记－北京市
－英文②城市－可持续发展－研究－北京市－英文 Ⅳ.
①K820.81②F299.271

中国版本图书馆CIP数据核字（2012）第040352号

Recovery of the Heart

Dialogues with People Working towards a Sustainable Beijing

心灵的回归：北京的未来在你我手中（英）

作　　者：Stephanie B. Tansey
责任编辑：李淑娟
英文审定：姜竹青
封面设计：贺玉婷
封面图片：华盖创意（北京）图像技术有限公司提供
责任印制：李一鸣　黄厚清
出版发行：北京　新世界出版社
社　　址：北京市西城区百万庄大街24号（100037）
总编室电话：+ 86 10 6899 5424　　68326679（传真）
发行部电话：+ 86 10 6899 5968　　68998705（传真）
本社中文网址：http://www.nwp.cn
版权部电子信箱：frank@nwp.com.cn
版权部电话：+ 86 10 6899 6306
印　　刷：北京画中画印刷有限公司
经　　销：新华书店
开　　本：787×1092　　1/16
字　　数：200千字　　印张：15.5
版　　次：2012年8月第1版　2012年8月北京第1次印刷
书　　号：ISBN 978-7-5104-2634-6
定　　价：48.00元